Copyright © 2010

The Agents Road Map:

11 Insurance Agents Show How They Got Their Agency To The Next Level, Made More Money And Took More Time Off

By Michael Jans

"This book is absolutely fantastic. It is so chock-full of value that you can't put a price on it! These phenomenally successful agents have peeled back the curtains on what they have done to reach this pinnacle state in the industry. They reveal step-by-step their best kept secrets, and share with the world instead of just keeping them to themselves. Anyone who reads this will discover exactly what it takes to explode their practice and the fastest way possible."

Brian Anastasio
State Farm
Albuquerque, NM

"Let's face it, times are tough right now and the economy isn't dong handstands, but some agents are thriving! – If you are tired of hearing how bad things are and want to see what is possible, even in these trying times – Read the book! Stop buying into all of the negativity and start implementing the strategies outlined in this book!"

Kevin McEwen
Hillcrest Insurance Agency
Mount Dora, FL

If you have any inspiration to better yourself; to improve your agency, your employees, your relationship with your clients, community and family then you must read and learn from these 11 insurance agency leaders"

Chris Raders
McGregor Insurance, Inc.
Ocean Shores, WA

COPYRIGHT © 2010 By:

All rights reserved. Except as provided under U.S. law, no part of this book may be reproduced in any way without permission in writing from the copyright holders.

This book contains IPS proprietary content and is provided to you by Insurance Profit Systems™ pursuant to the IPS Subscription Agreement located at
http://www.quantumclub.com/ipssubagree.htm

Additional Copies of this book may be requested by visiting

www.QuantumClub.com
www.Insurancemarketingrebel.com

Preface

Something just changed. You may not know it quite yet, but it did.

It all started the day you ordered this book, and the process will speed up now that you have it in front of you.

How do I know this? I was in your shoes. I'll never forget where I was in 1998 when I read a free report that I ordered off of a Rough Notes ad. I read the whole report, because I was fascinated by what this Jans guy had to say. As I dialed the phone with credit card in hand, I remember wondering if I'd look back at this time in my life when I made this step. Would it be a defining moment in my life? Wow! Was it ever!

No, I have nothing to gain from telling you this. Frankly, if you're in my area, I might prefer you didn't join the Quantum Club. I'm only writing this foreword as thanks to Michael Jans for the many ways he helped improve my business and my life.

Here's what Michael and the Quantum Club have done for me, and will do for you.
I guarantee it.

You'll quickly learn to stop doing things that don't advance you and your business to the next level. Things that don't make a lot of money. Things that you can pay someone else to do, and for a lot less than what you're worth. You're going to fire yourself as the chief cook and bottle washer, and get out of the kitchen. You'll use your knowledge, experience, and freed up time to drive customers to your business. You'll only work on your business, not in it.

You'll learn the marketing skills to acquire new clients, and in large numbers, not one at a time. You'll learn how to nurture these clients, and retain them. You'll learn how to get more business out of these customers from referrals, up-sells, and cross-sells.

Once you see how well this all works, you'll get a certain attitude. You'll have the confidence that no matter what the market throws at you, you'll make it. Hard market, soft market, fickle insurance companies, bad economy, lost a big account...it doesn't matter. Nothing is going to stop you from advancing to the next level. You'll always see opportunity. You will succeed. You just know it.

Freeing up time is not just great for working on your business. It's huge for you and your family. Now you can have a life. Spend more time with the family. Take more vacations. Do what you like to do. You'll stop living just to work.

Oh, and did I mention you'll make a lot more money. Imagine that. You work less, take more time off, and make more money. I know that concept is strange, but it's true. Believe me, that's exactly what happens.

All these ideas, skills, and techniques will come from two sources, the first being Michael Jans and his Insurance Profit Systems. This guy is a genius, and he's surrounded himself with incredibly talented people.

You'll be blown away by the amount of in-depth material and systems they've developed. And it doesn't get stale. They just keep improving and adding more stuff. That's why I've stayed around for over eleven years.

The second source of inspiration and ideas are the members of the Quantum Club. Not only are they gifted and successful entrepreneurs, but they're willing to share their ideas with other members. Proof of that is the book that's in front of you. When you join, you'll experience it when you go to events. The time spent with other members is absolutely priceless. Where else could you go, and find people in your industry willing to share their closely guarded secrets?

Join QC, and look me up at one of our events, and tell me if I was right. I know what the answer will be, and you're welcome.

When the student is ready, the teacher will appear. Well, the teacher is here now. He's right in front you. Now it's up to you.

At the beginning, I said that something just changed. It's your life. It's the life of your family, employees, and co-workers. Do you feel it?

Dave Cornish, President/CEO
C & G Insurance Agency
Woodridge, IL
Class of '98

Introduction

Our firm recently conducted a survey of insurance agency principals with the following true or false statement:

"The last 12 months have been among the challenging in my career."

I was expecting a strong "true" response. But I didn't expect to be bowled over. 94% responded by saying that statement was true. 94%!

And this was a cross-section of agents throughout North America. All sizes. All shapes of agencies. Personal lines. Commercial lines. Urban, rural, surburban.

I've been consulting, training and coaching in the industry for almost 20 years – and I've never seen pressure on the retail agent like I see today.

We've seen other industry's get slaughtered over the years. And not just the "horse buggy manufacturers" from decades ago.

I asked for a show of hands to the following question at one of our Closed Door Conferences recently. "How many of you used a travel agent to book your flight to this conference." One hand went up. The other 124 people booked their own flights through the Internet.

I booked my travel through an agent...perhaps because I'm the godfather of my travel agent's daughter!

Will the insurance agent go the way of the travel agent – decimated in numbers?

At least part of the answer to that question lies with the insurance agent.

The Second Great Insurance Agent Crisis

This is not the first time the agent has been under extreme pressure. A few short decades ago, there were over 80,000 independent insurance agencies in America. Today there are less than 40,000.

What happened? Big forces.

First of all, the industry went through one of the longest "soft markets" in history. As premium rates shriveled, so did profits.

Second, pressure was put on the agent to "run like a business" – not a private practice. The industry virtually required the agency to operate with the new technology of an "agency management system." Many of the smaller or older agents simply weren't ready to make the jump.

Third, carriers increased the premium volume requirements, forcing many agencies to merge.

One force or another – or some mixture of the three above – put many agencies out of business. Or pushed them into a merger or acquisition.

That was the First Great Crisis .

Now, we're on the precipice of the Second Great Crisis. In fact, I'd say we're well beyond the tipping point.

What's happening today that will affect agents in the months to come?

- **The Internet.** 32 million online quotes in 2008. Almost 39 million in 2009. I'd say that's *beyond* the tipping point, wouldn't you? And – even worse

– 71% of those quotes went to three carriers: GEICO, Progressive and esurance. 63% of online consumers went to the Internet to shop their insurance. Only 26% called or visited a local agent. 35% of online consumers who have not purchased insurance claim their like "like to do to so in the future." The consumer is already there. The agent is, sadly, far, far behind. (Note: agents who are serious about exploring the power of the Internet for their agency should investigate www.agencyrevolution.com.)

- **Mega-Competitors.** GEICO and Progressive alone spent well over a *billion* dollars in advertising last year. I recognize that many agents represent Progressive – but do you really think that "Flo" – the bizarre girl in white on TV – is pitching the retail agent? Not when she wags her finger at the consumer and says, "Did you shop online?" And when he says, "Yes!" she shouts, "DISCOUNT!"

- **Long soft commercial lines market.** Six years of progressive pricing discounts – and counting. This will go on longer than we wish, as always.

- **Economic downturn.** The Insurance Research Council estimates that one in six drivers will shed their insurance because of the economy. Payroll is down. Businesses are going out of business. Written premium was down. All because of the down economy.

- **Health insurance legislation.** This will affect agencies differently, depending on how much income they generate from benefits. And, of course, how the legislation "shakes out" in the real world. But you can certainly count on this: income won't go UP because of this legislation.

I'm not alone in predicting that the coming years will see some "thinning of the herd." Winterkill, as it were. Agents *must* look to the next few years and plan and act *now* to survive.

Over the years, I've been blessed to work with many of the most successful agents in North America. Even some in South America, Europe, Asia and Africa. And I've seen struggling agents rapidly take control of their agencies – and leap-frog over normal growth plateaus, quickly dominating their markets. It pleases me – professionally and personally – to think I've played some part in their success.

In this book, I present eleven of those agents to you. And they will share with you precisely how they implemented the strategies and principles that we espouse in my company – through Quantum Club and other programs – to reach goals that were important to them and to their family.

You will see how they installed processes in their agency that transformed their lives and business in six key areas:

1. **Marketing:** the attraction, conversion, optimization and retention of clients, through creative and reliable processes.

2. **Team:** building "The Gifted Team" and aligning all internal activities to support and accelerate the achievement of agency goals.

3. **Time:** gaining complete control over the use of time, allowing the agency principal and other team members to fill time with strategic, high leverage activities.

4. **Sales:** installing internal processes, including scripting, management, measurement and coaching, that maximize sales at every point of contact.

5. **Auto-Pilot:** engineering efficient internal processes that "run" the agency, transforming it from a "private practice" that relies on the daily involvement of the agency principal, to a reliable *business* that operates at a high level of profitability.

6. **Leadership:** the creation and delivery of an inspiring vision of growth, with the business plans, models and strategies to achieve it.

Years ago, I was introduced to the strategy called "standing on the shoulder of giants." The most expensive way to achieve success is trial and error...hacking your way through the jungle –when you could take the shortcut that's already proven. Why not stand on the shoulders of these giants, who will show you precisely how to achieve the agency of your dreams?

Grant Davis built a multi-million dollar insurance brokerage and is ranked in the top 1% of financial planners and life insurance agents in the world. He has authored two books, produced multiple sales, financial planning and risk management training seminars. Having overcome huge losses in 2007 with the collapse of the California contractor's market, Grant recouped the money through aggressively implementing Quantum Club™ principles and tools in a very short period of time. He was easily recognized as one of our recent Best Year Ever finalists with over $5 million in new premium!

Billy Proudfit – formerly a network engineer in the telecommunications industry he never thought he would join the family business. After the loss of some major commercial accounts, Billy found Quantum Club™ and the tools necessary to build out new niches, train his staff, and take the family business to the next level. Along the way he became a Best Year Ever finalist for his outstanding achievements and implementation of systems, tools, and strategies within his agency.

Claudia McClain is the winner of the IPS Best Year Ever Contest in 2007 and principal and founder of McClain Insurance. Claudia will show you how she implemented high profit client nurturing and retention strategies to help her business grow. Since joining Quantum Club™ in 2003, Average monthly new business writings are up 53%, revenue increased 47%, and profits increased 73.2%. Claudia has been able to work fewer hours per week and spend more time with her family, knowing that her team and her agency will run smoothly in her absence.

Eric Most is Co-owner of Most Insurance and Independent Insurance Agency with 4 locations in the Tampa Florida area. He has implemented many strategic marketing approaches, including using Public Service Announcements as a way to get free publicity and to help people find homeowners insurance, a very important issue in Florida. Delegating and empowering his employees has also been an important aspect of the changes, and have allowed Eric the free time to complete an Iron Man competition.

Glenn Agoncillo is a Principal at a $40 million agency. Glenn's agency only had an average of about 1.25 policies per client in 2007 and he knew they could do better. He dedicate himself to improving the business and he set ambitious goals for himself. His agency's client list has jumped to 2,352, an increase of nearly 500 in a year. Even more impressive, their number of total policies reached 7,544, an incredible leap of over 5,000 policies from the previous year.

Gordon Sorrel has been the Principal of Texas Insurance and Financial Services for over 3 decades. He and his team have mastered niche marketing. Receiving endorsement from his affiliates has given his the credibility of being the expert in the niche. He does about ninety-percent commercial and ten-percent personal lines. A large section of his commercial business is crop insurance, with close to $7 million and nearly $7 million plus in commercial, and close to $3 million in personal lines.

Jim Janasko owns the agency started by his father over 50 years ago. Jim has instituted more efficient systems, and he has learned to delegate to the rest of his team. He now has the opportunity to focus on marketing and growing the business, instead of on the mundane day-to-day details. Jim has implemented a nurturing and retaining program for the clients he values and giving back to his community through charitable contributions—which he has been able to incorporate into his thriving referral program.

Joel Zwicker manages multiple agencies for AA Monroe Insurance, a $30 million agency, at an office in the Annapolis Valley in the sparsely populated province of Nova Scotia, Canada. He has developed new techniques he learned from Quantum Club™ and has tweaked and adapted several key marketing strategies to his region which has significantly increased his business and as a result he has opened another office.

Shaun Irwin is the owner of three businesses in addition to his insurance agency in Minnesota. He started implementing Quantum Club™ strategies that allowed him to get out of the drudgery of day-to-day operations and focus on the aspects of the business he most enjoys, marketing. He has learned the importance of investing in his employees to make sure they want to continue working for him and developed a unique employee-nurturing and retention program to help accomplish that.

Lee Hendrie founded his agency in 1966 in Orange County, CA. His agency currently has 4 offices with revenue in excess of $3.5 million. He has a clientele of over 12,000 split 24% commercial and 76% personal lines. Lee works only 26 weeks a year in California and spends the other 26 weeks with his family in Colorado.

Jamie Brown is legendary within the State Farm world and for good reason! Jamie was the #1 Auto Agency with Sate Farm in 2005 and 2006. Jamie has been a Lifetime member of the President's Club since 1996. Jamie is a 5 time State Farm Trophy Winner and in Check Point rankings in May 2010 Jamie ranked top 5 in auto and fire.

I believe that your agency is at the cross-roads...because *every* agency is at the cross-roads. Those who will thrive are those who *choose* the future. And the strategies that will work in the future. They are not the same strategies that worked for the previous generation...or, for that matter, the ones that worked in the most recent years.

I applaud these eleven agents for their success. Also for their generosity.

If your agency and its future is important to you – and if you're reading this book even this far, I believe it is – please welcome these ten agents into your life. They will show you shortcuts to the agency of your dreams.

For many years, this was a relatively easy industry. With the right strategies in place, it can be extremely lucrative. The path may not be easy for some. It will require change. And a serious commitment to business. The days of complacency are over.

But the future is in your hands. Let these agents – and the strategies they employ – take you to the future of your dreams.

Michael Jans
Bend, Oregon

"Our retention rate went up over 5 points in one year. It was 84.78 last year. This year our retention ratio is 89.27. What does this mean to our bottom line? Try $25,000. The state average for the company's agents was 86%. We outpaced the average by 3 percentage points. This stuff works."
~Tammy Lesueur, La Pine, OR

"Michael, I purchased a program from you "High Impact Marketing" in 1996 and started an agency in 1998. I recently sold it to a bank on an approximate $4,000,000 package. Much of my success came from using your program."
~William Loose, Langhorne, PA

"QC completely changed the way I look at my business. I've put my agency on Auto Pilot which has freed up my time for high leverage activities. Revenue is up 72% over last year. Thanks to Michael and all of the Quantum Club Members who have helped me."
~Lisa Sherer, Auburn, CA

"Just got my final numbers for 2000. My book of business is up 41% and my total personal book of business is now just under $600,000 in combined P&C / Benefit commission. The business that has been sold but not booked in 2000 almost equals my sales targets for 2001 and it doesn't include referral business already in the pipeline! Michael, just when I thought it could not be done, you have hit the bull's eye again. For the fifth straight time I expect to increase my P&C Sales by 30% or more."
~Bill Reynolds, Western Springs, IL

Table of Contents

	Pages
Grant Davis (Commercial)	19 - 38
Billy Proudfit (Commercial)	39 - 57
Claudia McClain (Personal)	58 - 83
Eric Most (Personal)	84 - 105
Glenn Agoncillo (Commercial)	106 - 122
Gordon Sorrel & Leigh Ann Johnson (Commercial)	123 - 150
Jim Janasko (Personal)	151 - 172
Joel Zwicker (Personal)	173 - 203
Shaun Irwin (Commercial)	204 - 229
Lee Hendrie (Personal)	230 - 264
Jamie Brown (Personal)	265 - 287

Grant Davis: Commercial lines in California

Grant Davis, a Quantum Club™ member since 2007, started a new commercial lines agency in 2000, handling mainly the construction industry in California. He was very successful at first as a result of a boom in the construction industry. However, in 2006, when that boom turned to bust, Grant's agency started to lose money very quickly. He knew he had to do something to turn his business around, so he joined Quantum Club™. Now his agency is extremely successful, and his story can serve as a great lesson of how to thrive even in a time of economic crisis. He attributes this success to three main factors: learning and utilizing marketing, implementing proven systems and having access to the community of Quantum Club™.

IPS: Hey Everybody! My promise to you is that you are going to get some real meat and potatoes out of today's conversation. I feel honored to be interviewing Grant Davis, who is a straight-shooter, a great guy, one of the most ethical brokers that I have had the privilege of working with, and a very high achiever. Grant, let me first say "hello" and thank you for joining us. I have actually changed the name of this seminar. It was called 'How This Agent Generated Six-Million Dollars in New Premiums in the Last Year,' but apparently we received an updated figure through our program consultant the other day, so it is an added figure and is now 'Seven-Million, Five-Hundred-Thirty-Eight Thousand Dollars in New Premiums in the Last Year.' I know everyone is going to be anxious to hear how you have done this. Grant and I have talked at some length about this, and what I have asked Grant to do is to give away as much as he possibly can. Let me start by giving everybody the big picture about some of the things we are going to be talking about. For starters, just to put this into perspective, what we are going to be sharing with you are some of the key elements that Grant has used. These strategies will allow you to attract prospects into your marketing funnel, to convert prospects into clients, to optimize those relationships so they generate the most revenue per client, and then to retain your clients as long

> "…four corners of marketing: delivering a big promise, demonstrating proof, clarifying exactly the proposition is, and then answering the question that people are asking, "how do I get it and why should I do it now?"

as you possibly can. For those you do not convert, put them into a 'lead warming system' and they go back into your attraction funnel. Part of the optimization process is to generate referrals; put them into your attraction funnel, and for those unfortunate souls who we do lose from time to time, we want to put them in to a 'lost souls process.' We will be talking in some length and in some detail about how Grant applied the principles that we talked about in each of those different areas. I am going to give you a little background on Grant and then ask him how he did what he did. Between the years 2000 and 2005, he grew his agency from scratch. Is that correct, Grant?

Grant Davis: Yes. We left an exclusive situation in January of 2000, so they kept theirs and we started new.

IPS: *So you started new in 2000 and added twenty million dollars in premiums, so you saw a tremendous amount of growth, and that was during a boom time in the California construction industry. Am I correct about that?*

Grant: Yes. It was a good time because they were building fast and the availability was a hard market for construction, so we had some unique knowledge and abilities that allowed us to leverage that.

IPS: *So you were able to ride a strong growth curve in the local or regional economy. In the year 2006 you got lazy, and the year 2007 is when it probably really scared you because you lost close to a million dollars in commission...*

Grant: ...and joined Quantum Club™! I had to do something!

IPS: *What I promised everyone is something that will give them some real meat and potatoes on what they can do, so this is what I felt was so interesting about your story. One of the most valuable lessons we can learn from your story is how to rebuild during a time of economic crisis – like you did when the California construction industry really went down the drain. A lot of your business was construction and that went away. So Grant, if you would, just take thirty seconds and tells the story of how we met.*

Grant: I was replacing some outdated computers in Southern California, so I was sitting in front of the TV and playing on the internet, looking at the Quantum Club™ website. That was a Friday night and I had probably looked at it for twenty hours by Monday morning. It was really interesting. There was a great WealthBuilder™ interview in there with Lee Hendrie. I was afraid to stop looking at it, because it could not be real, so I started downloading and looking at things, and I got into a manic state. On Monday I found out I could join, so I joined.

> "This is our general plan; every agency needs processes with which to attract prospects into their marketing funnel, and they need processes that convert those prospects into clients."

IPS: *Let's take a closer look at the past plan, and then I want to look at a few of the things that really worked well in your agency. This is our general plan; every agency needs processes with which to attract prospects into their marketing funnel, and they need processes that convert* *those prospects into clients. For the clients or prospects that you do not convert, you need some type of an automatic 'lead warming system,' and then they go back into your attraction funnel, back into your conversion funnel, and hopefully they become clients. With your clients you want to optimize relationships, so you want to generate maximum revenue per customer and the maximum number of policies per client; you want to generate testimonials, and you also want to generate referrals. The referrals then go back into the attraction funnel, get converted and optimized and become clients like everyone else. You then, of course, want to retain those clients as long as you possibly can. For those who do fall outside of your client base, you want some kind of a process to reactivate the lost souls. Grant, when you and I spoke the other day, you said there were two really big breaks for you, and they were marketing and systems. You said that both changed your life, so I am going to ask you to walk us through those two things. When you put marketing and systems together, you wind up with a marketing business where not only does the agency run well technically and take care of the clients in regards to their insurance, but you also have the systems that track them, retain them, track your numbers, nurture your clients and cross-sell them. Let us start with marketing. You had indicated that one of the things that was a big insight for you were the 'four corners of marketing:' delivering a big promise, demonstrating proof, clarifying exactly what the proposition is, and then answering the question that people are asking, 'how do I get it and why should I do it now?' So this was big for you, and you have been a great sales person for a long time; I mean, you added twenty million dollars in premiums in five years. What was the big insight for you with these 'four corners?'*

HIGH IMPACT MARKETING

Grant: A little self-examination. So if the steps are 'Attract, Convert, Optimize and Retain,' I was really good at converting in a private practice model. Anyone that has been in insurance for a number of years, like I have, will know that that is all you were trained to do. We were not really trained to attract, although cold calling is how I was trained, we were not really trained how to do it in a systematic way. Sometimes you call marketing a 'tack on system' and it did not even exist; it was something we just played with. At one point, prior to joining Quantum Club™, I was trying new things and trying to broaden the business, and I even sent out seventy thousand flyers one time and we didn't even get one phone call. I remember talking to one of my staff people and said, "You know, I could have written our phone number on a piece of paper and someone would have called to ask why they were getting my phone number in the mail." It is quite a trick to send out seventy thousand flyers and have not one person call. The first thing that I learned is what is supposed to be in an ad I have been trained in insurance and in professional sales courses, and none of them tell you just the basics of what is supposed to be in an ad. Here is your USP (Unique Selling Proposition) formula checklist, and that is how you get their attention. Number one: you have to have a unique headline and unique selling proposition, as this checklist demonstrates. You go through it and figure it out. It is not about just saving money; you have to be very specific to the group of people you are talking to and figure

> "That was the other thing we get from Quantum Club is the systems and the process designers."

out what is going to grab their attention. You have to get their attention before you can go anywhere else. The second thing that happens is, after you get their attention, you have to tell them 'what the deal is.' You have to give them proof using testimonials. You use other clients in the same niche that say 'Hey look – here is what we did!' That is the social proof. The proposition number three is 'What is the deal,' and it is 'If you call me, here is your offer.' We use phone numbers and fax backs, and that is actually fun because instead of getting a call you run to the fax machine to see what you have. These are people that are ready to go. After QC and about two thousand flyers, you get a four or five percent response. That is a little tough, too, if you do not have systems. That was the other thing we get from Quantum Club™ is the systems and The Quantum Process Designers™. If you think about sending two thousand flyers and getting a 4.7% response rate and someone has to handle 90 responses, that is a challenge inside of your agency. That is a lot of people that want to talk to you, and if you do not get to them quickly, you can lose them. So on our flyers, the right hand side is the testimonials; the left hand side is how you get it and what the deal is; the bottom is my phone numbers; on the backside of these is a fax back with a couple of quick questions. [FORMAT OF FLYERS]

IPS: *And if anyone wants to see these flyers, you have uploaded many of them into the Quantum Club Navigator™.*

Grant: Yeah, one of the things that is understated about Quantum Club™ is the community. I am getting much more than I have given. The ability for other members to share their information is huge; that is what kept me on that computer for twenty hours.

IPS: When I talked to you last week or the week before, you told me that you had just completed one week where you sold $160,000 in new premiums, and that was done off of a different campaign where you were only sending ten letters at a time. Tell us a little about that one.

THIRD PARTY ENDORSEMENTS

Grant: Basically, I have a client write me a testimonial letter because I make a lot of promises, so I need new clients and clients that have been with me for a while to say that I do exactly what I say I will do. When I get a good one of those in a niche that I want to develop, I ask my client if it is okay if we turn it into a third party letter and I mail it directly to my list from them. I ask them to restate their testimonial but to direct it more to a person. At first, I sent out a large amount of those and I could not keep up, so I just send out ten at a time now and wait for the response. I usually get one to two responses to the letter. I have had times where I sent up to 100 and had to make a few phone calls to ask about them receiving the letter just to test and tweak a little bit. I went on an appointment from one of these letters and, when I got there, the client wanted to direct. I wanted to go over my presentation, though, and explain how I wanted to

> "...One of the things that is understated about Quantum Club is the community; I am getting much more than I have given. The ability for other members to share their information is huge...."

do things. He just was not interested, so I explained that now was not the time to work on his account, which offended him, but if he could not do things my way then there was no sense in doing it. He thought I was an idiot, and I could tell I offended him. I wanted to do it my way, because I know my way works. Shortly thereafter, we were at a Rotary meeting and I saw my client. He went out of his way to find me and we discussed some things. This was lucky that the conversation happened and the next day I got a call from the guy.

> "We ask for referrals as part of the process...."

IPS: Am I right that you are now limiting the mail to ten of these per week?

Grant: Ten at a time; I could do more in a week than ten, but I have not. I cannot handle it. I only want to sell about two accounts this size in a month because it is a lot of work. This month we got five. Two of them came back to back, so I have everyone on overtime and going nuts trying to keep up with all of this.

[handwritten: TIMING OF LETTERS]

REFERRALS

IPS: Now, in addition to your lead attraction systems that we just talked about, you have also created a referral generating system. You really did not have one before, so tell us a little bit about what you are doing to get so many more referrals now than you used to.

Grant: It starts by doing business differently. I would say that I very seldom talk about insurance or use the 'I' word at all in anything we do. So it is not about referring an insurance agent or broker or getting insurance referrals.

We do referral rewards, like we promote and give away Starbucks cards, we put people's names in for a drawing and we do 'adopt a teacher' where they can send in information. We have helped Science and Gardening and Shop classes; they just tell us what they want the money for and what they would like to do. We fund a lot of those ourselves and each time we get a referral, we put more money into that. We also put our clients' names in for a drawing at the end of the year. It is not a lot but it is a little 'thank you.' <u>We ask for referrals as part of the process,</u> so when I am making my presentation and showing letters of recommendations, I tell the prospect that my simple objective is to service their account to the point where I will ask for and you will be happy to write a recommendation to tell all of your friends about me. If it is anything less than that, I have not done my job and they can give their account to another broker.

[handwritten margin note: ASK FOR REFERRALS]

IPS: *We know that when you get a referral and a testimonial, they are more likely to stay with you longer, anyway. That is a strategic retention strategy, as well.*

Grant: Definitely—when you ask someone to write it down and they actually write down what you did for them, they are feeling a positive emotion towards you.

CLOSING THE INBOUND CALL

IPS: *We just talked a lot about how you have been closing the big elephant accounts; in addition to that, your agency gets inbound calls that do not go to you. This is information I think I got from you months ago – your staff closed almost four hundred thousand dollars in commission on inbound calls, and they did that without you. I wanted to mention that because if anyone is thinking they should* *not go after the huge elephant account like Grant is, the same processes work and they need to be given some of the tools, systems, and scripts so that they are capable of closing that inbound call.*

SCRIPTS

Grant: A big mistake a lot of people make is not using that script filter; that is huge. If you leave it to each one of your staff members, you can have twenty different presentations to the same types of clients. If you use a script, you have a plan. If you know your numbers and you can see that one person's closing ratio is less than another person's closing ratio but they are making the same amount of calls, we can look at how the script is being delivered. If you do not have a plan, though, then you cannot tweak anything.

CROSS SELLING

IPS: *I want to talk about cross-sales, because you have also done a really good job the past couple of years going from one policy to multiple policies per customer; in fact, you said a few moments ago that you no longer sell one policy; you want to sell the account. Tell us a little bit about how you did that and how the CSR's do that as well.*

Grant: I took your Domination Theory Marketing™ Conference and then I expanded my

> "Instead of me making all the decisions and everyone coming to me with all the problems, we used The Quantum Club Process Designers™"

thinking again with the Summit. If you define what it is you are going to sell, think about being a salesperson and sell something, you are successful because you have made your sale. By defining what it is we are going to sell, that is all we sell. When someone says 'yes' to me, I do not just sell them a policy; <u>I sell them an entire account based on packages and services.</u> I am following Domination Theory Marketing™ and I built it all out. It works.

IPS: We have a cross-sell worksheet on the website that we developed that demonstrates how you can take this exact same customer base, in this case it is an agency we worked with several years ago that had 3,000 customers and was generating half a million dollars in commission income, and increase the number of policies per client. We designed a series of marketing campaigns and processes for them that increased the number of multi-policy customers from the same customer base and went from about $474,000 in commission income to $949,000, so they doubled the size of their agency without adding any customers. I really like to share this spreadsheet with people because it is a real eye opener. You can input your own numbers and develop an assertive scenario and an aggressive scenario. When you share this with your key people, they really get it in black and white. It becomes crystal clear how much value that customer base has when they are fully optimized. We also have the retention part of customer relationships; Grant, you have done a really good job at increasing your overall retention. We have another spreadsheet, called the Easy Millions™ spreadsheet and it is another eye opener. We have seen that if you have a million dollar agency and you bump your retention from 85% to 89% for example, the cumulative additional income per agency is in the multiple millions of dollars. Most agencies do not have an action plan that is

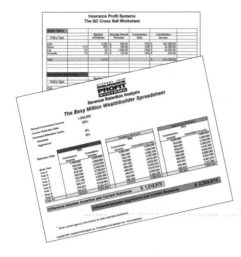

designed to capture that lost income, so I congratulate you, Grant, on your ability to do that. The other thing I wanted to jump to is that you said that you had two really big breaks: marketing and systems. Tell us a little bit about how that has affected your agency.

HOW TO IMPLEMENT PROCESSES

Grant: Instead of me making all the decisions and everyone coming to me with all of the problems, we used The Quantum Process Designers™. It was a year ago or so when we were struggling with it when I got a package in the mail from you: The Quantum Process Designer™. I did not even read it; I just handed it out and told my staff to duplicate it and make it happen. We started making processes for everything. When a process fails or breaks, we see what step failed and change it for the better. When we talk about systems, this is another system we follow. There is a form that they fill out about what went wrong, how they fixed it, and what they suggest. I delegated it to three key staff people, and they pretty much run the office and handle all processes now; we have made a nice recovery because of that. I have been able to focus my attention on building sales and marketing because they handle the day-to-day things pretty well. They also went through your CSR Mastery Program™, and that put them in line with my thinking.

COMMUNITY

IPS: You mentioned that you had three big things that really changed your life: one was marketing, two was getting your agency on systems, and three was the opportunity to join with a community of marketing geniuses, Quantum Club™. I am going to say a few words about that, and Grant you can add to it if you would like. In my experience, it is possible to very rapidly reengineer an agency so that it becomes a marketing agency like Grant's is, and it requires a different way of thinking about the industry and a different way of thinking than what the industry normally adopts in our culture. Instead of having to chase prospects, you can reorient your agency so prospects can run to you, that is if you understand the four corners marketing, niche selection, and market research so you can identify what their dangers and opportunities are that you can present to them. Then the agency can become simpler to run the more complicated it gets, but I think a lot of people are afraid to get to that next level. This is one of the reasons that industrial researchers have indicated: people and a lot of entrepreneurs do not grow because they are uncomfortable getting to the next level, but our experience is that the next level can actually be less complicated. I mean, you're happier. Right, Grant?

> "Because you get to work on your personal gift and delegate through Auto Pilot Control Program™ all of those things that really do not need to be done by the agency principal."

Because you get to work on your personal gift and delegate through Auto Pilot Control Program™ all of those things that really do not need to be done by the agency principal. Grant, you indicated that when you get more clients you can actually take more time off and your career can be more fun. As the years go by, some people kind of lose the fire in their belly and they are no longer doing the stuff they love to do. My experience is that this happens when they haven't built an agency on systems; the most important, most exciting, and most lucrative systems are the ones that focus on the <u>attraction, conversion, and retention of clients with the highest possible long term profit</u>, which is what my definition of marketing is, and building that on a proven process with reliable results. Good marketing pays for itself. So let's take some questions now.

[handwritten margin note: DEFINITION OF MARKETING]

James: In the beginning you had said that these old fashioned passive marketing tools do not work, like the Yellow Book, but we have gotten a bunch of calls for my agency when we were with Yellow Book. In our area, I do not see how it is a bad thing that we do.

IPS: What we are seeing statistically is a ten percent decline in the usage of Yellow Pages every year, so you can imagine how that is going to compound over the next three to four years, and that is not my figure; that comes from independent industry research. More and more clients are using the internet as a replacement for Yellow Pages. Are you in the Yellow Pages this year? How many calls are you getting from that ad in a typical week?

James: Maybe one…

IPS: Do you know what your monthly cost is? Let us say you are getting four calls during the month; do you know what the cost of the ad is? One of the things I would encourage you to do is measure the ROI from all of your advertising sources. Maybe you are still getting an acceptable ROI, but the time is coming when you need to begin replacing that source, as a lot of other agencies have discovered, as a place to do business.

David: I am one of those agents that is feeling all the pressures.

IPS: I sympathize. I do not want to take that lightly. I consider this the most serious time in the industry.

David: I am in a suburb in Chicago, and am seeing that a lot of small and medium size businesses have a lot of pressure. If I were going to invest $1,000 or $2,000, tell me what would be one particular program that you highly encourage because it will get me at least some return, and I will join the club.

IPS: I will jump on that, and this is a little bit of a dangerous question because I should normally be consulting with you and finding out about the composition and makeup or your agency. How many customers do you have?

David: About eight hundred.

IPS: How long has the agency been around?

David: Since '68.

IPS: Do you have a document and referral process right now?

David: No, but we used to.

IPS: One thing that I would do, and this is generally speaking, is analyze your agency for additional policy opportunities from your existing client base and add a referral program on top of that. That is without even looking at your current retention trends. That is easy money. It is pretty reliable to say that the profitability of marketing to your existing customer base is 500-700% percent more than marketing to new customers. One of the most profitable ways to get new customers is from the friends and colleagues of your existing customer base.

> "I would invest the money and get on the site... we have all built out our business using Quantum Tools."

David: I am willing to spend the money, but get me on the right track to start. If the money starts flowing, I am in. I have insurance classes up the ying yang! What I am not good at is what you are good at: the marketing. I need that help to get me over that first or second threshold. So I do not make some of the stupid mistakes. I need something that gets me going and on the right track feeling positive and pumped.

IPS: The other thing we would be exploring is lucrative niche opportunities within your existing book of business. NICHES

David: We do have one particular good-sized niche.

Grant: Can I jump in for a second? One of the things that we touched on in Quantum Club™ is the tools, and one of those tools is the Mastermind Groups. I have a group of 168 people. Marketing is sales put in writing. Think about

[handwritten note: DO YOU HAVE A STORY?]

it, right now, in any one of those niches, there are eight reasons why someone should and must buy insurance from you today. Now prove it to them. In other words, I am talking about a <u>presentation book for salesmanship.</u> Once you have that, you have a story to tell. If you have a story to tell, you throw that into the marketing process and you will have people to tell the story to. You asked what would be the one thing, and there are a lot of things, <u>but one thing is your story.</u> How are you telling your story? What is your story? And <u>how are you marketing your story?</u> That does not cost you anything once you join Quantum Club™. My Mastermind Group is all about that; we are all about sales presentations and such. You get all of that and you will get the idea really quickly.

David: I hear you and I understand what you are saying, but you are up and running. Help me get off on the run. There is a lot of pressure right now: companies demanding this and losing customers left and right….

Grant: I am not trying to be overconfident, but I can probably have you up and running in 30 minutes on the phone by using Quantum Club™ tools and the Quantum Club Navigator™.

David: If this company sits with me for 30 minutes and gets me going, I am in. I just need someone to lead me through.

Grant: I would invest the money and get on the site, then send me an email and I will spend a little time with you. In my little group, we have all built out our business using Quantum Club™ tools. A lot of the people I work with have the same question; that is why I have a group, so I do not have so many individual calls. You are asking a great question, and I honestly believe that a 30-minute conversation and looking at the Quantum Club™ tools will show you it is there for you. You have doubt.

David: It is not that I do not believe you. You are taking me from an agency owner who is great at insurance and a good salesperson into a marketing world that I am not good at, or I am not as good as you guys are. I am not skeptical; I just do not want to go from step one to step four and skip two and three and then realize we screwed up.

Grant: That is what I was talking about with your story; that is your <u>scripted sales presentation.</u> What are you selling and why? Why should I buy something from you? Then that is what you market, a reason to tell your story; that is step one. Step two is building your marketing around it.

[handwritten: BUILD YOUR STORY]

IPS: I leave the next step up to you. I think you are asking a great question, and we would love to be able to work with you. Grant is very generous in volunteering his time; he is not being paid for this. That being said, I did promise that we would make this a one-hour call. I know people have other things they have to do. I want to encourage those of you who want to join to give us a call. We will answer your questions and share with you, in detail, what we can do for you, realistically. Grant, anything else you want to say before we sign off?

Grant: What that gentleman was asking for is exactly what is in the Quantum Club Navigator™; he just needs a quick guide to find it. He does not have to skip any steps; it is right in order. What you do and how you do it is right there. You say I do not get compensated for this, and that is not necessarily true; I just do not get money for this. As

I am helping other people, I am helping myself to do a better job with my group. It is a neat dynamic. As I help someone else put something else together I can see where mine can improve. I would encourage you to join, give it a try, and just jump in. I jumped in with both feet, and it was the best thing I ever did.

IPS: Grant, I want to thank you for sharing your story. If anybody has any questions, call us and we will answer your questions for you. I am hoping that some of you will choose to work with us. Thank you to everybody for joining us.

> "Quantum Club has not changed my life – children have changed my life. Quantum Club changed my agency so I'm more profitable and can spend more time with my children. Next to licensing, Quantum Club is the smartest money I've invested in my business."
> ~Kevin Foley, Freehold, NJ

> "Before the Quantum Club I worked 60 hours a week in the agency and had no idea why. Now I devote 8 – 10 hours a week to agency business and nearly doubled my personal income this year. Let's face it – there's only one place to go if you're a P&C agent who wants everything you can get from your business... Insurance Profit Systems."
> ~Joe Hagan, Jr., Birdsboro, PA

> "Quantum Club and IPS have enlightened our agency on management and marketing techniques ... <u>no one else offers this insight</u>."
> ~Gregg Germanos, Schaumburg, IL

Billy Proudfit: Commercial lines in Pennsylvania

Billy Proudfit, formerly a network engineer in the telecommunications industry, never thought he would be in the insurance industry. Six years later, however, working for his dad's agency, he has found his groove. After joining Quantum Club™ in 2006, with the help of fellow members and Quantum Club™ resources, such as the Gateway Discovery Process™, he started to streamline the agency and create systems to help his agency work more efficiently and increase profits.

IPS: *Hello everybody, glad you're able to join us. I'm very happy to have Billy Proudfit on the line with us. We are going to be talking about some of the ways that Billy has transformed his agency. As always for Quantum Club™ Members, you will have an opportunity to ask either Billy or myself any questions pertaining to what we are talking about here. Billy, I'm really pleased to have you on this call, I really appreciate it. So let's start at the beginning for people that don't know you. It's a good story. Tell us how you got into the industry and what your background is.*

Billy Proudfit: Well, I have to tell you that I'm an S.O.B., which is a son of a business owner, so I never thought I would be in the insurance industry. But it pulled me in about six years ago, and when I joined the agency my dad owned I worked as an agent, and that's all I really concentrated on for a while. That was pre-Quantum Club™, later I had a moment when I was learning about the future of the agency and that led me to the Quantum Club™.

IPS*: Life before the industry…what were you doing?*

Billy: I was a network engineer in the telecommunications industry. It was definitely a radical change.

IPS: *So you worked at your dad's agency—we have a lot of respect for your dad and he built a good business. But clearly there were some things that you felt needed some attention and transformation, so what were some of those?*

Billy: Well I know this is general, but pretty much everything. To break that down a little bit more, our main issue was that we didn't have many tools in place to track client activity and find out what was happening on a weekly, monthly or quarterly basis. We had no system in place, not just for getting new clients but also for keeping the ones that we have. Things were pretty haphazard, lacking any real structure…I'm sure a lot of Quantum Club™ Members have felt overwhelmed in that way and can relate. Basically, that's where we had to start.

[handwritten: TRACKING CURRENT CLIENTS]

IPS: So how would you describe the difference now? How is life? How is business different now than before?

Billy: Well it's kind of a cliché when I say it's night and day, but that's really how I feel. Now we have the tools that incorporate my vision and help communicate it to the agency and help everyone get on board. It's been pretty radical, though we still have a significant way to go. The difference now is that we have that vision and we know where we want to go, and that's very comforting.

IPS: Yes and as entrepreneurs, we usually have a very strong emotional relationship with the businesses that we run. How would you describe how your feel about your business and how you feel about the future now compared to before you joined Quantum Club™?

> "Now we have the tools that incorporate my vision and help communicate it to the agency and help everyone get on board. It's been pretty radical…."

MINDSET

Billy: Prior to Quantum Club™ I was an insurance agent, now I view myself as an insurance entrepreneur. It's really a whole mindset change about growth—it's not just one policy at a time, it's on a much larger scale now. It's been quite a change.

IPS: *Let's talk about some of the things that you did to make that change a reality.*

Billy: One of the first things I did was follow the advice of a lot of the veteran Quantum Club™ members. I went through and broke down what they said in Qmail (Quantum Club™ online discussion group) and searched the topics that were relevant to my situation. I would say one of the most helpful things I found, that has helped out a lot of Quantum Club™ members, was the Gateway Discovery Process™. It has the questions that need to be asked, and those questions can be uncomfortable, depending on the situation and the circumstance, but that was what really opened my eyes to what we needed to concentrate on.

IPS: *When you completed that, did you share that with your father? Was that a collaborated process or did you do that on your own?*

Billy: No, when I first did it; I did it all by myself and I realized that I didn't know everything, which kind of put me in my place. I had a little reality check—there was a lot I didn't know about the financials and about some of the servicing of the internal operations. That goes back to being an insurance agent and constantly looking at new business. So we broke down what we needed to do, then I went to my father and we discussed how we were going to improve the agency.

IPS: *So after you completed the Gateway Discovery Process™, you started to put an action plan together. What* *were some of the things that you focused on and what tools were useful for you?*

CLIENT NURTURING

Billy: I guess we are looking at our existing herd and it made me realize, wow, we were, I don't want to say taking advantage of these people, but we were <u>not doing anything to nurture them or giving them any reason to stay with us.</u> Taking the advice of other members, we put together a <u>monthly client newsletter</u>. It's kind of embarrassing to say this, but pre-Quantum Club™, just to get out a postcard or a client letter was a significant operation. It took a lot of work and a lot of coordination, so we started thinking, how can we nurture our clients? How can we segment our clients and figure out which ones are bringing in the money and which ones we want to keep?

IPS: Is that a new strategy?

Billy: Yes it is. Before, we were doing everything to keep even the smallest pain in the butt clients and we've changed that a little.

IPS: Besides the monthly newsletter, what else are you doing to nurture your clients?

Billy: We have also incorporated ZipDrip™ monthly messages. We send out birthday cards…and that's most of what I can think of off the top of my head. We also try to do a couple of nice things for our VIP clients. We are trying to put that into a procedure right now, to touch base with them at least once a quarter in a way that has nothing to do with insurance.

IPS: *Is the monthly newsletter going to all clients? Or only the Triple A or Double A clients?*

Billy: At first they were going to all clients because we just wanted to get it out there, but then we started paring down our list and taking some of our nonstandard auto clients off there.

IPS: *Did you go through a process of either firing clients or discouraging clients?*

Billy: Yes. We realized that we had clients who would show up in our office to make a payment with a bag full of nickels or never have their bill, stuff like that. I remember someone mentioned at one of the Boot Camps/Summit the letter that she sent about non-payments…that really helped get rid of a lot of people.

IPS: *So losing clients can be a good thing?*

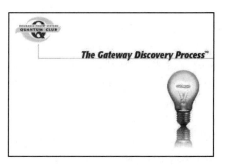

Billy: Yes, it made us leaner and meaner.

IPS: *So it was The Gateway Discovery Process™ that led you to really value the existing client relationships. When you start sending out the newsletter, usually there is a bit of a reaction from the market place because they've never had that before. Did you get responses?*

Billy: Absolutely.

IPS: *And with ZipDrip™, people often reply as well.*

Billy: Yes they do. What's interesting is that this agency has been around since the late 70's and all of a sudden this monthly newsletter starts showing up along with the birthday cards and tins of cookies for various occasions...I started receiving some letters and e-mails saying that this was the kind of stuff that we should have being doing from day one. And they were right.

IPS: What else did you learn from The Gateway Discovery Process™ and where else did you start putting attention? Often times when people realize that they are not fully valuing their existing customer relationships, they also recognize that they should be cross-selling more. What have you done in that regard?

Billy: We've done postcards, which we have success with, and umbrella policy campaigns that we've had a lot of success and fun with. We are just establishing a relationship with our clients again and we're able to sell umbrella policies to clients that have said in the past that they would never need or want one.

> "It is a great feeling knowing that you get through to somebody, even if it's just one policy."

IPS: Why are they saying they are doing it now? Are they responding to your marketing?

Billy: Yes, absolutely. It's a great feeling knowing that you get through to somebody, even if it's just one policy

IPS: Retention is up, cross-selling is up, so what else were you focusing on? What other discoveries did you make through your Gateway Discovery Process™?

Where else have you focused your time and resources?

TRACKING NUMBERS

Billy: We've done two main things. The first is tracking the financials. We started implementing new ways to track financials. That was one of the first things I did when I joined Quantum Club™. So now, on a monthly basis, I receive a spreadsheet with all the activities—all new policies, lost policies, cross-sells, everything.

IPS: You get a net policy count?

Billy: Yep, every week, and it is going up.

IPS: So it's going in the right direction.

Billy: It's going in the right direction and with that being said, now that we are tracking, I also realized that I needed to work on the high leverage activities. I needed to focus on growing the business activities and trying to get out of the day-to-day minutiae.

IPS: And who delivers your weekly net policy count?

Billy: We have a CSR/book-keeper.

IPS: And that person delivers that in a paper, hardcopy or email or an electronic version?

Billy: E-mail.

IPS: And it's on an Excel spread sheet?

Billy: Yes. So on Friday afternoon, if I'm at home, I can say, "Hey we are up 4 or 5 policies this week" and it makes me feel good, and plus there is also an outstanding invoice. We have a pretty significant agency book of business, so now we are getting that under control. We had stuff that was 60, 90 or 120 days overdue and now I know exactly who is late and why.

IPS: *I think this is valuable for our listeners. I'm curious about how much information goes on this piece of paper. Is it summary information like we lost 5 accounts, we gained 7? Or do you actually identify the name of the lost policy holders and the new policy holders?*

Billy: No…it's pretty much a summary. It's just an overall net, but if I see that we lost some accounts, sometimes I like to know who, so I will shoot an email back and ask.

IPS: *So it's the net policy count, and you also have an accounts receivable agent report? On that do you identify the names of the policyholders?*

Billy: Yes. Absolutely. I like to know that.

IPS: *OK…excellent. Let's go back to what you were talking about. So you also wanted to focus more on high leverage activities? And before, to some extent you were working on low leverage activities. What were they?*

Billy: Answering billing questions, or answering coverage questions. You know, to be quite honest with you, I look back and I wonder, "What did I do?" Why was I driving to the other side of Pittsburgh to meet with this client that did not justify the commission?

TIME OPTIMIZATION

IPS: *Have you ever completed a Mad Dog Time Optimizer™?*

Billy: Yes.

IPS: *What happened when you did that?*

Billy: It was an eye opener, actually. It was eye opening to say the least.

IPS: *Do you do that on a periodic basis?*

Billy: I used to do it...I would try to, maybe once a month, during the first year of my QC membership. It's probably more on a quarterly basis now, just to make sure that I am working on what I need to work on.

IPS: *If you lay one side-by-side with one you filled out two years ago, would they be significantly different?*

Billy: Absolutely.

IPS: *OK, so now let's talk about what some of your high leverage activities are.*

Billy: OK...that's what I enjoy talking about too. There were a couple of tools that I've incorporated that have helped out and one of the first things that I started using was the Laser Focus Planner™. I remember Quantum

Club™ members Ted Hamm and Claudia McClain always talking about the Laser Focus Planner™. I thought, "Heck! If it was good enough for them, then maybe I should be using this." So now that is my day-to-day planner...I've identified chunks of time for high leverage activities that I need to work on. Basically, I have appointments with myself to work on those high leverage activities like commercialized planning, niche planning, acquisitions, client nurturing, VIP client nurturing, my Internet presence and other websites and that kind of stuff.

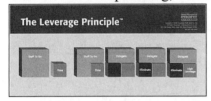

IPS: Do you use the 21 Big Chunks™ tool as part of the Speed Strategies™?

Billy: Yes I've incorporated that into the Laser focus Planner™, so now I have it written down and these are the chunks that I'm going to work on Monday, Tuesday, Wednesday, Thursday and Friday and that is consistent week to week. Now each day I have another little tool, the kitchen timer. I set that for an hour or 2 hours and use that time to work on client nurturing activities.

IPS: So in terms of your personal level of productivity...you're working on high leverage activities now, and that's established?

Billy: Yes.

IPS: Since you used the kitchen timer techniques, and I know we have trained on that at Speed Strategies™, have you noticed that your own personal level of productivity, focus and discipline is higher?

Billy: Yes, I do, and it's significant. There are times when I look at that timer and I think, "Oh my gosh, I can't believe there are only 14 minutes left," and that's a good feeling.

IPS: How long do you set your timer for?

Billy: I started off with an hour and I've noticed that I wasn't concentrating on what I needed to be concentrating on for the full hour, so I cut it back to a half an hour. Now I think I've gotten a little bit better so now there are times that I can set it for about an hour and a half.

IPS: When you go into it, you know how much you have left, which can really help with focusing.

Billy: Yeah and what's even better is that I share this schedule with my team, so they will know on Monday morning I'm working on our niches, and that way between 9:30 and 10:30 I'm not going to be interrupted with phone calls. This is displayed on our Internet sites so everyone can see and get used to the weekly rhythm. I've also helped establish a weekly rhythm for them where we've blocked out 3 hours per week for them to work on high leverage activities in relation to their jobs. If I'm benefitting from this, why not share the wealth? We are in our second week into blocking time for the team and so far, so good.

IPS: *Let's talk about the team for a moment. Do you have people with you now who were with you prior to Quantum Club™?*

Billy: Yes.

IPS: *And how are they responding to the changes?*

Billy: They are very positive; they have seen the change and they are excited with the direction we are going in. Any time there is a change involved, especially if they were here even before I was here, I'm forever grateful for their willingness to try it out, and they have really accepted all of the stuff that I have brought to them. What we are going to do is significantly different than what we have done in our first 30 years of existence.

AUTO PILOT CONTROL PROGRAM

IPS: *I'm excited to hear that. You're also using The Quantum Process Designers™, and I know you have been paying attention to the Auto Pilot Control Program™. So what's going on in your agency with that?*

"Before, there were some steps that we were avoiding, or we were just missing something… Now everyone is responsible for doing at least one [Process Designer] per week."

Billy: Well this is not a quick fix and it makes you think things from the beginning all the way through to the end. Sometimes it creates a little more work, but it's worth it. Before, there

were some steps that we were avoiding, or we were just missing something. This time last year, I was trying to get everyone to do The Quantum Process Designer™, but we were a little too haphazard. Now everyone is responsible for doing at least one per week. We meet every Friday, individually, and talk about The Quantum Process Designer™ from beginning to
end and if it incorporates a couple people, then we bring them in as well. Now they are going onto our Internet sites.

IPS: *OK, excellent. In terms of your future vision of the agency, I know you have a much stronger sense of clarity about what the agency will look like. Tell us a little bit about that and how you came to that.*

Billy: I guess I was just thinking about where we want to be in 5 years and, once again, I jumped on the coattails of other Quantum Club™ members, like Claudia McClain, from sitting in on her presentation last year. It's still my vision, obviously, that I want to grow, but how are we going to do it? Once again I had to ask difficult questions, like how are we going to get there? Can we do it? Which niches are we going to concentrate on? Can we develop other niches? It requires the complete dedication of not just me, but everyone involved. It's identifying not just the marketing activities, but also the internal side; we have to have total control, just to keep everyone's sanity in place. I did a little diagram showing what we do and what we do for our clients, and I presented it to the team and told them this is how we are going to do it.

IPS: *Okay, and can you tell us a little bit about your niches?*

NICHES

Billy: Yeah…we concentrate heavily on the contractor's niche here in Pennsylvania and on the personal lines side, we are doing the parents/teen drivers niche, and we are really excited about that. My personal lines CSR's are excited about that, because we are a heavy commercial agency and a lot of the attention is on the commercial book, but now we're trying to develop another niche. Then once we get that up on relentless automatic marketing, we will try to develop another niche.

IPS: *I assume you had contractors in the book before you became a Quantum Club™ member?*

Billy: Yes.

IPS: *Since you've joined, what kind of media are you using to attract them and cross-sell them, or convert them or retain them? How do you communicate with that niche?*

Billy: We use ZipDrip™ a lot, and the newsletters.

IPS: *Do you have a separate ZipDrip™ account set aside for contractors?*

Billy: Yes

IPS: *Do you write those? Or do you just rely on our commercial lines ZipDrip™ messages?*

Billy: It's a little bit of both. When I see something relevant in the newspapers or the trade journals and the industry's magazines, there's a good chance they are going to see it, but I'm going to take the chance to let them know that I'm reading what they are reading, just in case. We are doing a lot better job of just being in front of them; as we all know, contractors are a slightly different animal, so their needs are a little different.

IPS: *What are you doing to attract contractors?*

Billy: Well, you know, that's what we are still working on. We can get a lot better in that area. Now we just mail postcards to people on our list, and we are in the process of trying to set up a separate referral program, just for our contractors, independent of what we are doing for our agency.

IPS:*So I'm assuming your have a referral program in place, is that working well?*

Billy: Yes it is, and pre-Quantum Club™, I couldn't even tell you if we got referrals.

IPS: *Often I will ask "How many more referrals are you getting now?" and sometimes, people just don't know because they don't know how many they used to get.*

Billy: Yeah, I was one of those guys.

IPS: *But I assume intuitively, you can usually tell when you are getting a lot more.*

Billy: I can say with definitive proof that we are getting more, a lot more.

IPS: And now you know when there is a referral, and I assume you know who they are coming from and you have a systemic reward process?

Billy: Yes we do. We like those people and we like to reach out to them a little more and do something a little extra special for them. A card saying we're thinking of you, or maybe cookies or something like that.

IPS: Billy, we covered what I wanted to cover and I think it's pretty easy for me to see from this conversation why you've been successful. I mean, it's evident that now you've got some clarity in your thinking and you have strategies that hit the most important parts of the agency. Your recruiting, retaining, and niches are all improving, you're nurturing your clients, and it sounds like you're building systems for both internal operations and future marketing.

> "I thank you and the Quantum Club™ members. I couldn't have done it without their advice and resources."

Billy: Absolutely.

IPS: The results, and the reasons for the results, are obvious. Congratulations to you.

Billy: I thank you and the Quantum Club™ members. I couldn't have done it without their advice and resources.

IPS: And now you're passing advice onto others who are listening.

Billy: I hope so.

IPS: *That's what our community is all about, so I thank you for that. Before I see whether or not we have any questions, Billy is there anything you want to add that we've missed?*

Billy: I think there is a Qmail posting today encouraging us to take massive action. It's easier said than done, but you know if you can focus your time and use it wisely, on things like those high leverage activities, then that massive action is a lot more obtainable.

IPS: Anyone with questions for Billy? This is a rare opportunity to speak with an agent who has made a big difference in his own business. Russ is our first caller.

Russ: Cross-selling from your commercial niches to your personal lines, are you doing that?

Billy: Not nearly enough and that's interesting that you mentioned that, because we were just talking about that last week, about how we can do a better job on that. Naturally, some of our commercial books would come to us because they like the way we handled their business, but we never really had a way or we weren't consistent enough to ask them for their personal business, and we're going to do a lot better job in doing that now.

Russ: I'm always curious on what we are doing and what others are doing, so that's why I was looking to see if you are and how your were doing it.

Billy: I'm sorry Russ, but I can't give you anything really too specific right now. It's on the list to do.

IPS: Our next caller is Claudia.

Claudia: Hey Billy, congratulations. Great interview…I just had to step in here and tell everybody what an amazing member of our Nexus mastermind group that Billy has been. He is one of the newer members to our group, and he is always there with generous contributions and ideas and support. He'll send us emails to remember things that we may have said we had promised to do to hold us accountable, and so this was just my quick testimonial and heads up to everybody that Billy has just been a wonderful Quantum Club™ member and we really appreciate it.

IPS: Well, two of our winners of the Best Year Ever contest in a row. How about that?

Billy: I thank you Claudia. You have been a great help to me. I can tell you that.

IPS: Billy, once again, I want to say congratulations to you and thank you for sharing.

"We have been trying for five years to figure out a different way to write more insurance easier, faster, etc. We firmly believe that we have found the key through IPS."
~Karen Slaugh, Grand Junction, CO

"Michael's marketing ideas are great and exciting and will be like lighting a booster rocket to our agency."
~Bill Herbert, Englewood, CO

Claudia McClain: Personal lines in Washington

Claudia McClain, a Quantum Club™ member since 2003, won the IPS Best Year Ever Contest in 2007. She is the principal and founder of McClain Insurance in Everett, Washington, and has implemented some very impressive client nurturing and retention strategies to help her business grow. Their new business writings went up about 48%, their revenue increased 13.2% and profits increased 14.1% since joining Quantum Club™. Additionally, the average number of policies in the agency went up by 9.4%. One of the most rewarding results of these changes is that Claudia has been able to work fewer hours per week and spend more time with her family, knowing that her team and her agency will run smoothly in her absence.

IPS: Hello everybody. I'm really thrilled about this conversation because I finally get to talk with Claudia McClain from Everett, Washington, the winner of our 2007 Best Year Ever Contest in which she was awarded the IPS BMW Z4 Roadster. I think she and Natalie drove that all the way from Chicago to Everett. How was that drive, by the way?

> "Winners of the Best Year Ever competition show how they used and implemented IPS principles, strategies and techniques that have create a successful agency and personally satisfying life."

Claudia McClain: It was absolutely awesome. Enjoyed every second of it.

IPS: We saw some pictures and they looked fantastic. So she drove home with a BMW, and we cut a check for her team members for $10,000. I think that was an important part of the reason that Claudia participated. She really believes in Building A Gifted Team™. From what I hear, they enjoyed getting that check.

Claudia: Absolutely. Natalie is in Germany right now, in fact.

IPS: Oh really? She got to go? Great. Well, Claudia has been a Quantum Club™ member for about four years. I can almost always count on Claudia to be present at a Closed Door Conference, and to be sitting up near the front and taking notes, and then when I see her again, she's *implemented a few important strategies and her agency keeps going in the right direction. I am thrilled to have Claudia on the line. At the end of our conversation, we will open this up so you can also ask Claudia any questions you might have. Claudia first of all, thank you for joining us. I'm going to ask for a little background first. I think so many people were thrilled that you won the contest. The contest is set up with some very strict criteria. A guest panel reviews the submissions that are submitted by our entrants. Then we answer some background questions. When the judges get down to the deliberation, which takes four or five hours, we leave the room. I think it's a great process and I think we had a great panel that did a terrific job. I did get a chance to interview them afterward. It was a tough decision, there were many good participants, but it was a decision that they arrived at unanimously. One of the reasons was that it was so obvious that the team was involved and motivated and inspired, so my hat's off to you on that, Claudia. You have a great team, and we all know great teams come from great leaders. They're not self organizing, so you are doing something right there and I think that was a real tribute to you. Tell us about the agency and how you got into it.*

Claudia: I started my career in retail, working for Sears Roebuck and Company teaching Sears telephone sales reps how to cross-sell. So when you called into a catalog store and wanted to buy their detergent, my job was to convince the people on the phone lines that they should buy a pair of underwear or something, whatever was on sale. I quickly realized that retail would probably be a pretty difficult career if I ever wanted to have a family. I was only about 22 at the time, and I decided to look into financial services and then got involved with personal lines insurance. Our agency was founded scratch in 1977.

IPS: *Who started the agency?*

Claudia: I did. It was 100% personal lines, and at that time, the agency allowed me to be a mom also. My kids had their study room in the back of our office for a number of years. The agency grew as my family grew, and we now have a staff of four and a half in our office, four licensed agents and a college intern, and we represent four major carriers and several niche carriers. We have an annual premium volume of about 3.75 million.

IPS: *Tell me a little about what has happened in the last four years since you've been a Quantum Club™ Member and how that's different than it was in the last 25 years or so.*

Claudia: I would say that since Quantum Club™ everything has changed. It has been a complete transformation. Not only of our operations, but also of our philosophy for how we approach the business. I think this year is when all things Quantum actually came together. I was sitting in the room, sitting on Qmail, watching people post and learning from so many generous members, but I will be the first to admit that I was one of the slower implementers. This was the year we got a team together. We went through a 50% transformation of our team in the last 18 months, so once we had our team together and got them to buy into Quantum Club™ ideas, Nick went to the Personal Lines Super Conference and all of our team members are in the CSR Mastery Program™. I started using the Team Member ROADMAP™, and used the Ultimate Agency Blueprint™ as the focal point for our team meetings. Once we did that and began to implement we developed more accountability as far as our goals went. Then the other things all fell into place. The Client

Nurturing, the Marketing on Auto Pilot™, the Niche Marketing, they all fell into place.

IPS: *Somewhere along the line you made the decision to enter the contest. Was that the first year for you to enter the contest?*

Claudia: It was the first year. I had signed up in past years, but had not executed. But this year it was a combination of being involved with the Quantum Club™ Mastermind Group, and we made the commitment to each other that we would enter the contest and then honestly, when I put the team prize out there it had a major impact. As we went through some staffing changes at the beginning of the year, I began thinking we are just not going to have a story to tell, and yet I kept telling myself I had to at least give this a shot. Because if the team had even the remotest possibility of that type of bonus money, they deserved it. So we had a team meeting and talked about it, hired the right person to fill the empty spot and went forward from there.

IPS: *What was the impact on the agency when the team arrived at the decision to participate in the contest?*

Claudia: It was amazing. It helped us to become much more focused, much more efficient because we had a lot more things we needed to get done. It increased the enthusiasm with the team. We were always thinking about the contest. We talked to our carriers and they got excited, and would bring up either ideas or additional co-op money or just support. In general, by the time we were ready to put our submission together we were able to really put together a package that included a lot of testimonials because people had known we had been working on this for a number of months.

IPS: *What was the reaction among the carriers when you won the contest?*

Claudia: It was unbelievable. Some fellow agent friends who were in the audience were actually calling some of our carrier marketing reps whose cell phone numbers they had on Saturday night to let them know. The carriers have been most excited, most generous. One of our carriers, and I really do feel that it's a direct result of the Quantum Club™ honor, has invited me to serve a two year term on their national agency council. I am sure that wouldn't have happened without The Best Year Ever Contest. So thank you.

IPS: *That is terrific. Well let's get down to business here. So you had a pretty good year last year. I think you said that you doubled your previous year's new business activity—how did you phrase that?*

Claudia: Our new business writings were up about 48%. We are a seasoned agency, so an increase on almost anything is difficult. Prior to our commitment to making this our Best Year Ever, we had been going along with 3%,

4%, 5%. We increased the revenue in our agency by over 13%, 13.2% I think it was. Profits were up 14.1%, and the average number of policies in the agency was up 9.4%.

IPS: Your policy per customer count was up.

ORGANIC GROWTH

> "Our new business writings were up about 48%. We are a seasoned agency, so putting triple digit increases on almost anything is difficult."

Claudia: It was up as well, by 6.2%, and that makes a large emphasis on organic growth last year, so our focus was to try to increase the number of clients in the agency through referrals. We wrapped up our referral program and revamped it a couple of times to make it work. Then the second part was to increase the number of policies per client, to increase both retention and revenues. We did that with a strong emphasis on cross-selling and an increased emphasis on client nurturing. We have been attempting to come up with a formula that allows us to increase our average premium per policy. With the soft market that has been a little tougher to do, but we are putting some initiatives in play in the coming year to target the higher revenue personal lines accounts like families with teen drivers, and additional nurturing to the top 20% of our client base to increase referrals from higher caliber clients.

IPS: You have a terrific little formula that you call the "five by five by five" program. Tell us what that is.

Claudia: That actually evolved from working around the Ultimate Agency Blueprint™ with trying to come up with an outrageous goal for the office. In our case if we are only increasing by 3% or 4% per year, the biggest outrageous goal that I could think of at the time was to double our agency size in five years—although now our goals are changing, because we've been successful, but at the time that was our goal. To double the agency size in five years would require 15% growth each year for five years. We worked backwards from there and came up with the "five by five by five" which is basically 5% increase in the number of actual active clients in the agency. The second 5% is the average number of policies per client, and we exceeded that at 6.2%. The next 5% is the average premium per policy. Our largest Personal Lines carrier took a 5% rate decrease last year, so we are even on that number, but we didn't grow.

REFERRAL PROGRAM

IPS: Nonetheless you did increase your profits by 14% and your revenue was up 13.2%, so you were pretty close anyway. So let's dig into the details here. You indicated that one thing you wanted to do was get more referrals. Tell us about your referral program.

> "Our referrals have increased by over 50% since implementing that particular strategy."

Claudia: Well for referral programs, I think you have to tweak it for your own market and figure out what works. We started with lottery tickets and then a monthly prize. The lottery tickets weren't generating a lot of enthusiasm so then we went to a gift card. That's what we do now and people seem to really like it in our market, and keep in mind that a lot of our marketplace is educators and families. Our current referral thank you program is that if we receive a referral, we send a $10 Safeway Your Choice gift card. There is a specific reason we are choosing the Safeway Your Choice gift card. It says Your Choice on it and our agency tag line is Your Agents of Choice, because we are an independent agent and we represent many companies. So we give them the Your Choice $10 gift card and then we donate $10 to the school of their choice. We send them a thank you card that includes the return postage postcard for them to write down on the postcard what school they would like the donation to go to. Our referrals have increased by over 50% since implementing that particular strategy.

IPS: *So you've made more than one change. You've got the Safeway card, plus a $10 contribution to a school. When did you implement this change?*

Claudia: It was in September or October of last year, so it was just as we were coming to Boot Camp/Summit.

IPS: *So we are going to see even more referrals next year.*

Claudia: That is the plan.

IPS: *So this is a postage paid postcard and they just write down what school?*

Claudia: Yep, then we accumulate all of those postcards for a month and total up the amount, write a single check to each school or PTA and list who the referrers were so they will get some recognition.

IPS: *I suspected the special reason you selected schools is your categories contribution?*

Claudia: Yes. We have always marketed as a personal lines niche to educators, employees of schools and school districts.

IPS: *It's probably your largest niche, is that right?*

Claudia: It is, without a doubt. We hope we will get the others to grow to that level, but we've been working that niche for the whole time we've had the agency.

IPS: *One of your carriers really has its roots in that niche.*

Claudia: Correct. In addition to the referral thank you program, which puts the emphasis on donations to the schools, during Back to School time in our newsletter we developed a thank you gift for teachers, which was a branded insulated lunch bag with an Office Depot gift card, some granola bars and some highlighting pens. Just anything we could think of that a teacher would like and put it all in this really nice bright blue branded lunch bag that said Educators Just Deserve Extra Credit and had our agency phone number on it. Then in our newsletter we ask our clients to nominate their favorite teacher and we would send the favorite teacher a gift. The clients are thinking "oh what a nice thing" and they send in all these nominations, some of them with really lovely things to say about the educator and then we created in-house a nice note card saying this gift is coming to you from John Jones or whoever and McClain Insurance. We either hand delivered the lunch bags or mailed them, depending on how far away the school was from our office.

IPS: When did you implement that?

Claudia: That was Back to School, so that was in September of 2007.

IPS: Well, that's outstanding. What kind of reaction did you get?

Claudia: The clients were thrilled. They said, "How nice to be thanking the teachers." The educators themselves were very appreciative and we generated a number of excellent referrals from that, which will continue to grow. Any time now that we write an educator, even if they haven't come from that referral stream, we send them the lunch bag as a welcome to the agency gift.

IPS: Good, very creative. Claudia, you've mentioned that one of your goals was to get more referrals from your top 20%. What are you doing this year to make that happen?

SPECIAL EVENTS

Claudia: We already started the idea of setting up events within our office, or events that our clients are invited to, that are added value. We will be focusing those invitations first on the top 20%. For example on February 12 we have a jewelry appraisal event where I've hired a jewelry appraiser to come into our office for the entire day and the clients will bring their jewelry and receive a written appraisal while they are here so they won't need to leave their jewelry items. Then she will forward to them through the mail a formal copy with photos, which of course we will then make sure we schedule that jewelry on their homeowners policy, generating additional premium. We sent out just one notice in our last newsletter for it and all of the slots for that day are filled up in half hour increments. Of course we are going to have a half hour to talk with those clients because she's going to need the half hour to do the appraisal. During that time we've already started the process of lining up their account file. They don't know that this is what's going to happen for them, but we will do an account review during that half hour that their jewelry is being appraised.

IPS: That's terrific. How long is the appraiser there for?

Claudia: She comes in at 10:00 AM and she offered to stay until 7:30 PM.

IPS: Oh my goodness! So you filled up one half hour increments all day long.

Claudia: Yes. I think we have 20 folks already. Because we had overflow, I asked her if there was anything that we could do for those people that aren't going to be able to come in. She agreed to let us send out a $20.00 gift certificate against her regular retail price for an appraisal for anybody that either has more than one piece to be appraised or that just can't get in on that day.

IPS: What did you have to do to get her for the day?

Claudia: I had to pay her. So it will cost me about $800. But I've got a carrier that's going to co-op off of that.

IPS: You will walk away with more than $400. Hopefully you will use your camera to take lots of pictures and put them in your newsletter.

Claudia: You bet.

IPS: *I love that! Pictures with you with your arm around clients, and you'll put them up in the agency. Of course you will walk away with testimonials and you'll have some great displays for the office. Let's go back to the previous year when you won the contest. What were some of the other things that you did? What strategies have you executed that brought you the success that you had last year? For example, I'll pull one out, you said that you wanted to increase the number of contacts that you had with your clients. What did you do?*

CLIENT CONTACT

Claudia: That was huge for us because we had not been doing a regular newsletter. We had used ZipDrip™, we had used some postcards before, but we had really listened to all of the Quantum Club™ members that were strong advocates of newsletters and wanted to start that. Now we make contact with our clients a minimum of 18 times a year. That's done by 4 to 6 page newsletters that are sent out every other month. We produce them in-house. Natalie, one of my employees, is very creative and does a wonderful job of putting together the newsletter. We alternate the newsletter month with a mailing month, and the mailing could be either a specific postcard, or a letter or some other gift item to the client. Every month the client is

hearing from us with something that comes in the mail. In addition, I would say that 8 or 12 months a year they are receiving ZipDrip™ messages. It just depends, we may go to a full 12 months this year, but we were getting to a point early on that we thought maybe we were hitting them too often. They were getting ZipDrip™ messages, safety messages, and announcements from the agency on the events that we were having. One of them was the shredding event where we hired a shredding truck. One of our clients is a book author and we had a book signing and gave away children's books. We've done a number of community events that we always invite our clients to, such as Cinema Under the Stars, and Night Out Against Crime, which we partner with the Everett Police Department. Those have all been opportunities not only to participate in the community, but to also be telling our clients through the newsletter, postcard or a ZipDrip™, please come to this event we are one of the lead sponsors.

IPS: *Claudia when you look to the future, and you've already described some of the changes you are making, but what do you see as important strategic changes or strategies that you will implement that you didn't implement previously?*

Claudia: First of all, while I still plan to double the agency's size organically in five years, I am very interested in agency acquisition, which we have never done before. I am convinced that this is the time to be looking at that. So I will be attending the Agency Acquisition Boot Camp, and I am looking for opportunities for likeminded agencies to bring into our fold. In addition to that, I have not done the Emergency Contact Program, so that's on our plans for the first quarter along with an Automatic Response

Technologies (ART) announcement to make sure that people understand that it's coming and it's something important for them. I plan to also come up with a strategy to have some form of gift with that. I'm not sure if it will be spring flowers or flower seeds, but something like that to go with the mailing of the Emergency Contact Program. There will be a sense of reciprocity which will make them more likely to respond. We will be developing new niches. We are working on the families with teen drivers niche. Safeco came to us and asked us to develop the marketing for a condo unit owners niche, and we are working on that.

IPS: Good. Next please remind me, if you would, what your niches have been. I am asking for a specific reason because frequently people don't think of personal lines as niches. They think it has to be a commercial line strategy.

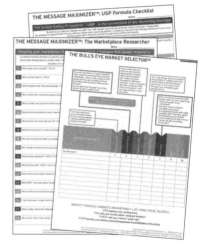

Claudia: Even though we have that niche of educators in our office, we never really identified it as something that we could market to. We were still just scatter shot marketing, yellow pages, and all the rest. It doesn't work in the current environment. An agency our size does not have the money to just send a mailing out without it targeting a specific group.

IPS: Right. You are not going to go up against Warren Buffet right now.

Claudia: Exactly. Our niches are educators and now earthquake is a niche because AllState and several carriers completely non-renewed their earthquake exposure. We have a niche company that does that very well. The Condo Unit Owners, the Parents of Teen Drivers, because our office is located in the home of the Boeing Dreamliner and the 747, we have a large number of clients on our books that are engineers. Engineers tend to be a very specific type of niche. They are very analytical folks so we developed certain strategies for working with them. Going forward, I'm realizing that we are very effective when we communicate by e-mail with clients. We are going to be looking at what we can do on the internet, and I can't say that I've got that completely fleshed out yet, but I'm looking at it. I realize that there
is an entire market out there that does want to come to our website to get a real-time quote. We are now beta testing the real-time quoting option on our website with four of our carriers.

> "I was away from the office in June for a Quantum Club™ event, and then in October for a Quantum Club™ event, and I had other things tacked on to either of those events so I was out both in June and October for almost half of those months, those very same months my team had their best months ever. So the lesson for me and anybody else wondering if this can be done- happily get out of their way!"

CLIENT RETENTION

IPS: Claudia, could you tell us a little bit about your client retention strategy?

Claudia: Our client retention strategies clearly have to do with increasing the number of policies per client and increasing the number of times we make contact with them. This year we tried to put as much of our client communication on auto-pilot as we could and we use our college intern to handle all of those automatic contacts or touches so that we know they go out even when all of us are busy with other things. We have a renewal letter program, the two-step welcome kit. With the renewal letter program, if there is a claim reported to us, we have a two-step claim follow-up series of letters that the intern handles for us.

> "This year we tried to put as much of our client communication on auto-pilot as we can and we use our college intern to handle all of those automatic contacts or touches so that we know they go out even when all of us are busy with other things."

IPS: Okay. I'm going to slow you down a little bit. Give us a few words about your welcome kit.

WELCOME KIT

Claudia: Our welcome kit comes in stages and we are now going to add a third stage, we just decided that yesterday. The third stage will be an e-postcard sent out to the client immediately, just thanking them for joining the agency. The same day we have a vinyl embossed file folder branded to the agency that is mailed out with a copy of their application and a welcome letter asking them if there is anything they have to sign and return to send it back, and we provide a return postage paid envelope. About 10 days after the policy is written, we have a vinyl pocketed folder that includes all of the contact information and this is, I believe, on the Quantum Club Navigator™ and anybody is welcome to use this. It includes everything from the contact information, who to contact, some overview information about their coverage and about our latest agency newsletter. The referral program is very prominently featured also because we want new clients especially, to know that that's part of what you buy into when you buy from us.

IPS: *Your renewal letter is kind of a program, and it has two stages to it?*

Claudia: The renewal letters, no, I'm sorry. It's the claim follow-up that has two stages.

IPS: *So when do they get the renewal letter and what makes it different than what they get from the average agent?*

Claudia: We were experiencing some issues with one of our carriers when some clients who had been with us the longest, had the best credit scores, and the cleanest driving record, were targeted for rate increases that in some cases were as much as 20% to 30%. The other clients were seeing huge decreases, but this particular preferred group of clients was seeing major increases. We actually started with a hand written note to the clients thanking them for their business, letting them know that their renewal would be coming shortly. Enclosing a Starbucks gift card, around here everybody loves that, saying, when you get your policy please enjoy your favorite beverage while you review your policy and let us know if we can help. Then we have more of a standard renewal letter that goes out that identifies cross-sale opportunities if we have just the auto, not the home at renewal. We are identifying what the savings will be if they brought the additional line to us. We've been doing that for a number of years. So I guess you would say there are two steps.

IPS: *Then the claim process?*

Claudia: The day that the client reports the claim, the CSR that takes the information and hand writes out a note, a descriptive that says we are so sorry to hear about your loss, here's our business card, you will be hearing from the company, let us know if there is anything we can do. Then again, it goes into suspense, and then within 10 days to two weeks they are getting a follow-up letter with a claim service report card. The claim service report card has been amazing. I am just amazed at the return on that. We are getting more than 75% of letters we send out back with reports of how their claim has gone. It's generally very favorable, but whatever they are we share them with the insurance carrier.

IPS: *The carrier gets a report from them too?*

Claudia: That's right.

MORE TIME OFF

IPS: *Claudia, before we open it up for questions, is there anything else that you want to add? Anything I've missed? I have one, two, three; I'm on my fourth page of notes. I'm still learning, you know.*

Claudia: The only thing we didn't talk about that you usually ask everybody else, is that you know that I love this business so much that I don't take as much time off as other agents do. I think it's really important to tell people that I have gone from working way too many hours, 60-hour weeks, to now working a more manageable 35-hour week. I am taking more time off to take vacations with my family. The very best thing I can say about all of this is that when I was away from the office in June for a Quantum Club™ event, and then in October for a Quantum Club™ event, and I had other things tacked on to either of those events so I was out both in June and October for almost half of those months, those very same months my team had their best months ever. So the lesson for me and anybody else wondering if this can be done- happily get out of their way!

IPS: *I have one more question for you. You indicated that you put together a lead warming strategy?*

Claudia: Right.

IPS: *Okay. This is for prospects that you were not able to convert into clients on their first call or first quote is that right?*

Claudia: Correct.

IPS: *So now you have developed a lead warming strategy that you got from Dominations Theory Marketing™. What are you doing for these guys?*

Claudia: Every quote is mailed or emailed, that is just a given in our office. So they've gotten that from us, and then the lead gets suspensed and within 10 days the college intern is sending out a follow up letter restating the fact that we'd love to work with them and sharing with them the carriers that we represent, including a page of testimonials. That gets sent out with another business card and then it gets suspensed again so that we are re-contacting that client, assuming that they haven't responded in those two groups that they may have bought somewhere else. The agent is going to be calling them too. In terms of the actual auto-pilot part of it, the lead is suspensed again for the fifth month if it's auto or the eleventh month if it's home. We will send another letter this time saying, last June we spoke with you about your auto insurance and we would like to talk to you again. Of course, we include a copy of our current newsletter so that they can see that maybe our agency is a bit different that other agencies in terms of the education aspect. Of course, every lead is put into ZipDrip™ too.

IPS: *So they are getting contacted just like a client all year long. Okay.*

Claudia: We put the good prospects on our newsletter mailing list, so we probably send out extra newsletters every time just to prospects.

IPS: Okay. Outstanding! Claudia, let's see if our audience has any questions for you. Okay, our first question is from Geri.

> "I looked at marketing, not as a budget expense, but as an investment."

Geri: Claudia, I have one question. It's just a little off track. Those of you who were present for her presentation know the penguin was part of her theme, her mascot. Could you describe the meaning behind the penguin?

Claudia: The penguin started because at Cinema Under the Stars, which is our family movie series, our featured movie that our team sponsored was Happy Feet. So as give-a-ways at Happy Feet, we gave out penguin socks that were branded with our web address and McClain Insurance. Anybody who is looking for socks as a give-a-way, I've got a great source. So we've been giving out socks a lot this year with the penguins on it. Another thing that came up throughout the year is that the smaller penguins all work together and protect each other against predators. We did some research on penguins and learned a lot and it has become the theme for the year.

Geri: Fantastic. It was absolutely clever the way you incorporated that on the tops of your cookies and your presentation cake that went to IPS, and the whole nine yards. I had the socks hanging in my office and I have another pair at home I wear every day. I am a supporter of the penguin and Claudia.

Claudia: Thank you, Geri.

IPS: Our next question is from Bill.

Bill: Hello, congratulations are in order, Claudia. You deserved it and you got it, and I'm just envious because I've always wanted a BMW…and I will get one! Claudia, I have a proposition for you, however, since you enjoy those 60-hour work weeks so much, I invite you to come over to the east coast and spend a month with me. So while you are here your agency gets bigger and you can help me do those 1001 things that you are able to do. I'm just envious, I really am. You are just a fantastic person. Organizing and the whole nine yards. I am just so thrilled that you got rewarded with $10,000 for your team and a car for yourself. I'm envious.

> "I think the key was first of all putting together a process designer for everything that you want to do so that you can put that process designer in front of anybody and say you know Joan is out today, will you get the renewal thank you out?"

Claudia: Bill thank you for that, that sounds like a win-win situation doesn't it?

Bill: Yes it is.

Claudia: Honestly, there really should have been 13 BMW's because I learned so much from each and every one of you that were up there on the stage, and I congratulate you. I hope you know how much I admire and respect everything that you shared with us.

Bill: Well, dittos.

IPS: Our next question is from Jeff.

Jeff: You have a lot of good ideas and I'm listening to those. We try to implement what we can and Quantum Club™ information is great. How many people do you use with the tasks that you were talking about? How many people does it take?

Claudia: Are you asking overall in the agency how many it takes?

Jeff : No just, you know, for the renewal follow-up, you mentioned something about an intern you're using, I believe, and you send out a quote and you do a follow-up and you are sending out a renewal letter and you have a Starbucks coffee card. How do you do that? Do you use one person only, or two people? Your mailroom?

Claudia: Good question, Jeff. I think the key was first of all putting together a process designer for everything that you want to do so that you can put The Quantum Process Designer™ in front of anybody and say you know Joan is out today, will you get the renewal thank you out? Bottom line in our agency, there are four licensed people, including myself. One agent does primarily new business and one agent does primarily customer service, but they both overlap and both cross-sell. One licensed agent who doesn't really function as an agent at all and that's Natalie. She was hired as an administrative assistant and then got her agent's license. She does an awful lot of the coordination of our newsletter, and some of our marketing strategies. The college intern who works on average about 15 to 20 hours a week, her role is to actually execute all of these autopilot things. The agents have a role of giving the suspense, and Natalie has a role of designing the Thank You cards for example. The intern has the role of actually getting it out the door.

Jeff: Wow. Okay. So now I know how many people it should take!

IPS: Our next question is from Glenn.

MOTIVATION

Glenn: Congratulations, Claudia. I have all these motivational sayings for myself and one of them is, what would Claudia Do? And I look at it every single day. My team always looks at me kind of crazy, like who is Claudia? My question to you is what motivational tools do you use to help your team see your vision?

Claudia: Oh, excellent question. I think that what I will say is that we take a lot of inspiration that comes from members like you, and inspiration from IPS. I try to read a lot so when I come across information that inspires me we share that with the team, or I will buy them all the book or whatever it may be. I think I am very blessed to have team members that after we went through the Team Member ROADMAP™ and kind of put the plan together, they share the ownership of the vision and really bought into it. They know if our agency doubles in size they are the critical group that will have made it happen and they will grow professionally and hopefully personally in the process as well.

Glenn: Thank you.

IPS: Okay we have time for one more brief question. What'll it be Joyce?

Joyce: We were looking at the budgeting that you would have Claudia on all the things that you were doing. I know that you mentioned that you had some of the carriers help with the costs of some things. But what was your budget like?

Claudia: I looked at marketing, not as a budget expense, but as an investment. I am looking at each individual item that we might be doing and evaluating it as we see the results. So I can't give you an actual dollar amount or percentage. I can tell you that I've got some carriers who are very generous with co-op. I know that last year I spent at least $26,000 in marketing but got at least half of that back in co-ops, at a minimum.

Joyce: Okay. That's all we needed thank you.

IPS: I think a lot of that is the philosophy and the paradigm of what a marketing dollar is. It's an investment, not an expense. Okay Claudia, thank you for your time and all your great advice.

> "The changes I made from what I learned from you are <u>worth $1.6 million in commission, first year</u>. This is dynamite. This is specific. This is stuff you can take home and use and put it in the bank. And where else are you going to find it? Nowhere else. All I can say is 'Thank you, Michael.'"
>
> ~Richard Crebs, Napa Valley, CA

Eric Most: Personal lines in Florida

Eric Most, a Quantum Club™ member since 2008, is currently on his way to owning the agency his father started nearly 40 years ago in Tampa, Florida. He never thought he would work for his dad, but he's very glad he changed his mind, as he has made some important changes to the agency and had a lot of success. The agency is truly a family business, and now Eric, his brother and sister all work for the agency. In a unique marketing strategy, Eric has also included features on his three-year-old niece in his newsletter and other agency publications. He has also implemented many other clever marketing approaches, including using Public Service Announcements as a way to get free publicity and to help people find homeowners insurance, a very important issue in Florida. Delegating and empowering his employees has also been an important aspect of the changes, and have allowed Eric the free time to get healthy, get in shape and even train for an Iron Man competition.

IPS: I want to welcome all of the Quantum Club™ members, new and old, to today's WealthBuilder™ interview with Eric Most from Tampa, Florida. When I first met Eric I noticed right away that he had a very fresh approach to marketing. Even though he was a relatively new member, I wanted to ask him a lot of questions. Here we are, a year later, talking about what Eric has implemented and learned from Quantum Club™. I think you are going to find that the benefits of Eric being here include two things: a lot of you might be on the sidelines of QC, and this might be an example of someone who was on the sidelines and jumped into the game. You do not need to have twenty-years of experience in the insurance business to be successful; after all, it is a business, and certain marketing principles are true no matter what you are selling, be it shoes or insurance. With that, I just want to welcome now, Eric Most. You remember when we first met, right?

Eric Most: I sure do. We met there at the hotel and a big group of us got together. It was an exciting time for me. It was kind of an 'ah ha' moment that occurred that day. It was a good time and it sparked a lot of growth and a lot of new missions and visions within our organization.

> "I am very, very glad that I got started because what I have learned now is that I was not wasting a penny with Quantum Club. It has helped me make bundles of money...."

IPS: How long had you been a member of Quantum Club™ before then?

Eric: I was a member for about two-years before coming to that first Quick Start Day. I got the "Quantum Club™ in a box," one of the conferences in a box, and looked at it at one point and thought, "This is great," but I slid it under my desk and it stayed there until I moved to a different office. It stayed there again until about two-years ago. This time, as you said, at the Closed Door Session in Orlando, I finally said, "I either need to get going with this or just completely drop out and stop wasting my money." I am very, very glad that I got started because what I have learned now is that I was not wasting a penny with Quantum Club™. It has helped me to make bundles of money, and I am thankful that I got going with different principles with Quantum Club™ and with different people.

IPS: *That is great. Before we get into all of the things that you have taken advantage of over the last 12 months, I really want to emphasize the point that it is hard to value what the Closed Door Meetings are about until you have been to one. Would you agree?*

Eric: Hands-down. To the people who are talking about just joining in, I have said and 100% believe that, if it is not too late, you should call and beg to be let in to the one that is coming up next week. Get a plane ticket and fly out there, because the time that is spent there is incredibly valuable, not only for the meetings we spend time in during the day, but also for the meetings with other Quantum Club™ people—people who have the same kind of mindset, people who are looking to grow, not shrink, in this economy. If you go to a normal insurance meeting, quite often you are going to find that you are talking to a bunch of other people who are down-in-the-dumps about the economy. If you go to a Quantum Club™ meeting, however, you have people that are stoked because they just implemented this new system, and this new system is bringing them much more money; they are talking about growing, not shrinking. The meetings have a two-fold benefit: first, you are learning these different principles, and second you are learning and networking with other top agents from across the country that have been in the same shoes that you have been in, and they can give you new ideas and bounce things off of them. I remember, this past October in Chicago, I was driving around the city with John Mason and a couple of other guys. I have since implemented some of the things that we discussed in that conversation, and it has been night-and-day in my agency since I have done that.

IPS: *Before we get into some of the tools, I want to talk about the referral program. But first quickly tell the listeners the background of your agency.*

Eric: We have been in business now for 38 years. My father started the agency as a Nationwide agent here in Tampa, Florida. Things went pretty well for him, and he hit some good growth in the early nineties by putting an office in a good location. When each of us kids got to our senior year in high school, he sat us down and did the money talk about going to college and coming back to work for him. We all said, "No," and I actually laughed in my father's face and said, "There is no way in hell I will ever work for you!" That was after I had already quit two jobs doing clerical work for him in high school. I am glad that I was humbled because, after college, I came back and asked for a temporary job, and he said, "Sure." After about a month into it, my eyes were opened and I knew that there was a really good business there that had a lot of potential. I said to my father, "I might stick around a little bit longer, Dad, if that's okay; maybe permanently." Last year we went independent, as many Nationwide agents did, and we moved over to the Allied Platform. I am here in Florida, and we absolutely have loved life in the independent world. Now, I have actually started taking ownership of the book and buying my father out. My father, my brother, and I are all in the agency, and I just hired my sister to work remotely for me from South Carolina, so I have the entire family in the agency now. I have four offices and approximately twenty employees. We are, predominantly, a personal lines agency. We used to do a lot of big habitation commercial, but that all went away during the hurricanes of '04, and we are now reinvigorating our commercial department. That is a little bit about us.

IPS: Let us go right into what people want to hear – the nuts and bolts – you have had some success with your referral program, haven't you?

REFERRAL PROGRAM

Eric: I sure have. I think that referral programs are one of the easiest things that people can institute, and it was the first thing that I tackled when I returned from that meeting in Orlando. I said, "Let's give this a whirl," and my brother and father thought I was nuts. I like the TV, and everybody was doing it, but I wanted to think of other things I could do. As you know, people in Florida like cruises, and cruises are relatively inexpensive and easy to get to here, so I changed from the normal giveaway on the referral program to a five-night Western Caribbean cruise for two out of Tampa. It costs me about seven-hundred-and-fifty-dollars, so it is significantly less than the cost of a big flat-screen TV. We gave away our first one this past year, and our customers love it. I also give each person $3 worth of lottery scratch-off tickets, and we do a drawing each month for a $50 gift certificate out to dinner.

IPS: *How long did it take you to actually implement the referral program?*

Eric: After I downloaded somebody's referral program off the Quantum Club Navigator™ and changed the picture of the TV to a picture of a cruise ship, it took about thirty-minutes to actually implement it, change it out, and start sending it out. We started by sending out flyers to all new customers and sending mailers to my existing customers. The nice thing with Quantum Club™ is that you have the ability to borrow from everybody who puts their tools out there, and that is what I did. I took it off the Quantum Club Navigator™, changed it slightly, put my name on it, and shipped it out.

> "To the people, who are talking about just joining in, I have said and 100% believe that, if it is not too late, you should call and beg to be let in..."

IPS: *Is this going out with your new business packet, or does your CSR actually ask for the referral?*

Eric: We ask for the referral, but we usually say, "Have you heard about our referral program where you can win a cruise for two?" We also send it out with all new business. We send it out in our New Customer Packet, and it goes out in every piece of mail we send to existing customers. It is on bright yellow paper so customers can see it; when they see that piece of paper, they know it is from me and they know what it is.

IPS: *With your new referral program and the customer packet, this is nothing new that you had to invent. It was already out there for you, it just needed to be tweaked a little bit, right?*

Eric: Absolutely! I downloaded it from the library; the library is a goldmine of gems. Most everything that I have done has been pulled from what someone else has developed and tested. I tweak it a little bit to reflect us, but it is so easy that I barely even have to think about things.

IPS: *For those not familiar with the Quantum Club™ Member Library, there are subcategories within the library on personal lines, auto, homeowners, newsletters, internal operations, Mastermind groups, referral programs, and the likes. Again, these are the tools at your disposal, so use them. Eric is such a great example of somebody who has jumped in and I am envious of his success. Another thing you have done that is worth mentioning is that you have taken these tools and added some personality to them. I do not think that anyone who would read this in a marketing handbook would agree with using your three-year old niece as a marketing tool because it might not get that much attention, but you have done things like this with your newsletter.*

Eric: First, I have to say that the only way I actually get my newsletter done consistently each month is because of BJ over at Quantum Club™. I use the AMD, Automatic Marketing Department™, and she sends me the newsletter each month. I tweak it a little bit, send it back to her, and she sends it out to everybody. I used to try to do a monthly newsletter and it went out about twice per year before, and it was not that good. I have taken an idea from another member who uses his dog in his advertising, so I thought,

"I have a three-year-old niece who is incredibly cute," and I wanted to add some personality to my newsletter. I took the stories on the front cover of my newsletter and moved them back farther in the newsletter, and I added an entire article called, "What's Dana up to?" That is my niece's name, and each month she is getting into some kind of trouble.

Designed to help Agents get things done. The AMD Program takes care of newsletters, cross-sell campaigns, holiday cards and voice broadcasts automatically.

It is written in a kid's handwriting font called 'kids first handwriting,' and I have gotten my brother to write the article each month in a kid's kind of language and reflecting how a three-year old thinks, so it is an absolutely phenomenal news piece. I put pictures of her doing different events; for example, last month she went canoeing for the first time, and there is a picture of her with her best friend, Midnight, her dog. There is also a picture of her flying a kite. She always foreshadows what will happen next month, and she asks the readers to check back with her next month. I have posted my most recent newsletter in the library, so feel free to take a look at them.

IPS: How do you explain the success of that little marketing tool? Did you ever anticipate it would work so well? What is the connection that it is making with your customers?

PERSONALITY MARKETING

Eric: One of the Cialdini principles we have heard about is that people want to do business with businesses and with people they like, so I needed to think of a method that my customers would really like. I figured what could be better than using a three-year old girl. They absolutely love it! I have customers that give feedback if I send out a piece of marketing that does not include my niece. They stop in and tell my Dad, "It is so neat to learn about your granddaughter." They are showing my newsletters to their co-workers and passing them around. Of course, I also include my referral program so that they know about it.

> "When I am ready to do a newsletter, it takes me thirty-minutes to sit down, to have it completely done…."

IPS: This technique is sincere, not phony, and it warms up your customers for other pitches you have planned for them down the road.

Eric: We are using her more and more, and we have her at different Customer Appreciation Days. People can come out and meet us, and they can meet Dana. The personality marketing is the key. I did not think it was such a big deal in the past but after being in Quantum Club™ and learning using your personal life works. Do something that sets you apart from every other insurance agent down the street from you.

IPS: *This is all done through the Automatic Marketing Department™ (AMD)?*

Eric: Yes, I cannot do it. My strength is not in thinking up insurance things to talk about each month. When I am ready to do a newsletter, it takes me thirty-minutes to sit down, to have it completely done, and to send it back to Barbara for printing and mailing to all of my customers.

IPS: What else has the Automatic Marketing Department™ given you?

Eric: We use the Holiday Card significantly. Those are the main two that I have used a lot, and I have used ZipDrip™ significantly.

> "I know there are principles in Quantum Club™ that I have not even gotten to, that I know would make my life easier."

ZipDrip™ has been a huge benefit for me in the agency; our customers really love it. What I have discovered about ZipDrip™ is that the key to it is personalizing you. Just as different people have said, I am not thinking of anything new. One Quantum Club™ member shared with his clients that he was going out to have a green beer on St. Patty's Day, and I used that same exact message. I received twenty-responses within twenty-minutes. They care about the personal messages more than anything else on the ZipDrip™. I have implemented those different parts with the Automatic Marketing Department™ thus far.

PUBLIC SERVICE ANNOUNCEMENTS

IPS: *I wanted to mention something that I found absolutely ingenious, and that is the free publicity you have encountered with the public service radio announcements.*

Eric: I just started doing some radio commercials, and that has been huge. While I was sitting there, some guy said to me, "If you ever have a Public Service Announcement (PSA), we are required to run that for free for you," so I walked over to his desk and said, "Okay, I am going to figure out one of these right now." Here in Florida, we have a thing called FMAP.org for homeowners. Because we have such a huge issue with homeowners insurance in Florida, there is a free public service to help you to find homeowners insurance. Insurance agents can sign up to be on this page free, and they get free leads from people who need insurance. I have fifteen-second spots running, and I purposely kept them at fifteen-seconds so that they would sound more like a public service announcement, throughout prime time during any week that I run any radio advertisements. They say something like, "Florida Markets: This plan was provided to help homeowners get insurance." The message then slows down and it says, "You can talk to one of their local agents, Eric Most, at…" and it gives my phone number. That is running free, and it gives credibility to the other radio ads I am running, and it is just getting my name out there. The calls that we get in from people who hear about that hotline are absolutely huge. As I bring radio marketing to other stations, they all have to run those public service announcements free.

IPS: *Do you have to walk into radio stations and say, "I have a PSA, so run it."*

Eric: You have to use marketing with them is what I have learned. I was talking with Clear Channel last week about advertising and, as long as I am doing any kind of ad, even if I do very few, I say, "By the way, I also have a public service announcement that I need for you to run for me free." They say, "Okay." They run it free for the entire week that I am advertising. You could even create the public service announcement for yourself, if you are smart, and you can set up your own hotline. I have not yet set up the voice hotline, but if I had a hotline for a free report, I can probably get that past Clear Channel or other radio stations, and they would approve giving that information out in a public service announcement.

IPS: *Again, many of the things that Eric is talking about today are in the toolbox on the Quantum Club™ website. You get the impression, from listening to you, that you have a lot of enthusiasm and that you are sincerely interested in sharing your success. Let us get to the point, though, that it is not a 'bed of roses.' There is trial and error here, too.*

Eric: You have to implement. Sometimes you sit there with a huge weight on you, and you just have to start implementing things. I have sent out some pieces that were not the best, and a lot of it are just things that I have not implemented myself yet. There are principals in Quantum Club™ that I have not even gotten to that I know would make my life easier.

IPS: *I have always found that it is much easier to do something the second time than it is to do it the first time.*

FREE UP TIME

Eric: That is absolutely true. I am finally getting to the point where I am doing a good job with "The Rule of 46™: Delegating or getting rid of 5% of the things I touch every month." As the principles says, "If you get rid of 5% of the stuff you do every month, then in a year you will have freed up 46% of your time to work on high leverage activities." The key, for me is freeing up your time to work on the business, not in the business, and that has been something that has been a huge process for me, and I have been slow going on the Mad Dog Time Optimizer™. I am just getting to the point where I am doing a good job with that, it is helping me to free up time and to focus on tasks, so I can get things pushed through and keep plugging along.

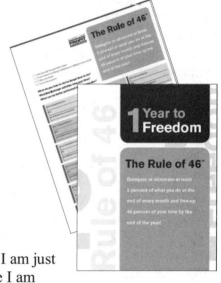

IPS: Let us shift from the marketing and return to your internal operations. Managing 20 people sure has its challenges from day-to-day. What have you used from IPS and Quantum Club™ to improve your internal operations?

Eric: One of the best things, frankly, just came to me as I was sitting here watching these different strategy calls with Michael Jans; he uses video. I have four offices within a 115-mile radius, so it is difficult to get to some of my offices. I now do a video for my employees almost every day, and I talk to them about updates and anything else that is going on. This is a way I have found that I can get the same information out to everybody, and it has really been a huge benefit for both them and me. They comment about the specific thing of the day, and that way I know that each employee has seen the stuff.

IPS: Can you give me the logistics of doing that video and getting it delivered?

Eric: I use a high-definition video camera on my computer, and just hit record for a minute or so, then upload it to our internal website. It has been a huge asset. I upload it to my agency website where all of my newsletters and forms are, so all of my employees can see everything that my customers see on a daily basis.

IPS: All that we have talked about has happened in the last 12 months, right?

"One of my biggest issues is time to train my staff, and that was one of my biggest negatives, so I have gotten Michael's CSR Mastery Program to do all of the training for me. I know that my employees are hearing the things that I am focused on, and it has been a huge success."

Eric: Yes, this has all happened in the last 12 months. I worked in the business for all of the time preceding that, and I was banging my head against the wall trying to get all of these things to move around. I have also used ZipDrip™ for my own employees to remain in contact and encourage them. That has been a huge benefit in managing my different people. I am in the Million Dollar Club here with Quantum Club™, and one thing we did last time I was there was discuss evaluating all of our employees. Grade them 'A' through 'C,' and if they are a 'C' or below, you need to fire them today. Get them out of your business. You need to figure out how to build 'B's' up to 'A's,' because you want all 'A' players. That was something that I did while we were in Chicago this last time; I literally graded every single employee. I talked about their 'plusses' and 'minuses' and what I needed to do to get them to be 'A's' or to move them along. We have moved a lot of people out of our agency. If people are not on board with Quantum Club™ principles and with what we are doing, then they need to move along and go to someone else.

CSR MASTERY PROGAM

IPS: Is the CSR Mastery Program™ part of getting that 'B' to an 'A?'

Eric: It sure is. One of my biggest issues is time to train my staff, and that was one of my biggest negatives, so I have gotten Michael's CSR Mastery Program™ to do all of the training for me. I know that my employees are hearing the things that I am focused on, and it has been a huge success. Right now, I have four employees going through it, my Account Managers, and they are learning, growing, and loving it. I sweeten the deal because I want them engaged so, while Michael offers the winner twenty-five-hundred-dollars, I am offering to match that amount if they win. They are looking at a chance to make five-thousand-dollars, just for doing their job. I have learned that you have to offer incentives to get the behavior you want, and I want them to be engaged by picking up all of the IPS systems, and what better way than to bribe them? It really is working.

IPS: *Another thing you worked on is The Quantum Process Designer™. You are also working on your internal operations with your processes.*

> "I have created a Prospecting Letter that goes out as soon as somebody calls in for a quote that has increased my closing ratio by more than 30 points."

Eric: I listened to this call with Sam Carpenter, read the book "*Work the System: The Simple Mechanics of Making More and Working Less,*" and realized that the biggest fault within our agency was that everybody was doing his or her own thing. There was a huge concern about efficiency and about not having a system in place. The people were not necessarily saying the things I wanted them to say. They were not bringing up my referral program or cross-sales every time, so we have gone through the process of putting everything that we do in our agency into The Quantum Process Designer™. We constantly audit it and make sure that we are doing things to the absolute best of our ability. That is also stored on our internal webpage so that all of the employees can see it from all of our different locations. "*Work the System*" is what has allowed me to free up my time so that I can work on more marketing and on growing the different visions of the business.

IPS: *You have had success within your agency, but it has freed you up to do things outside of your agency, which I think is interesting. You are training for something these days that was not possible 12 months ago. Can you tell us about that?*

Eric: I am training for an Iron Man Competition. I have been able to free up time for me to focus on more high leverage activities, both in the business and in my personal life. Before I really engaged in Quantum Club™, I weighed over 100 pounds more than I do now, and I could not even walk a block. These principles have freed up the time I need to be able to train for the Iron Man Competition, which is about 20 hours per week.

> "What I have learned is that as I have surrounded myself with better, higher quality employees, they actually do stuff a lot better than I would have done it. Things get done more quickly and more efficiently."

IPS: *That is the real success of IPS; it can transform a man's life like that. It is really a great thing to hear. Before we take questions, you should go over some details of your New Customer Packet.*

NEW CUSTOMER PACKET

Eric: I have a New Customer Packet and Prospect Quote Packet. I have a Valued Customer Packet that tells all about the agency. It gives a history of the agency and has pictures of my father, my brother, and me; it will soon include pictures of my niece, also. It has information on claims numbers for the different carriers, includes what they should expect at renewal time, and has information regarding the referral program. We also include our testimonial flyer, a welcome letter from the agency, magnets, pens, and other stuff to help people remember us. That goes out right after the policy has been written. They also get a letter from me to welcome them to the agency, and they get an introductory letter, three-days after that, from their Account Manager that welcomes the customer to the agency. I also have a Prospect Packet that I am using. I have created a Prospecting Letter that goes out as soon as somebody calls in for a quote that has increased my closing ratio by more than 30 points. I am just shy of 70 percentage points on my closing ratio. For every person that calls in, we close 70% of them. The letter includes the 28 reasons that they are crazy to do business with anybody else, testimonials, and my triple money-back guarantee. We also send a video email. We are using many different forms of media to get to our customers, and that has helped to close a significant amount of business. They also go into ZipDrip™ immediately, so they are getting auto-responders. We have started answering live calls 24 hours-per-day, seven-days-per-week, 365 days-per-year. That has been huge. I had an automated system that used a phone tree, and my customers hated it. I now have a doctor's messaging service answering my calls if my receptionist cannot do it, and they send me emails as soon as the call is over. They also transfer the emails to voicemail. That has been a blessing for us, and the customers absolutely love it. This is something that anybody can take part in. Send me an email, and I will get you information about the vendor I am using. He answers calls from all over the country.

IPS: Okay, our first question is from Blaire.

Blaire: I appreciate you taking the time out of your day to do this. I love the video idea. As far as referrals, what would you say generates the most excitement out of your current book of business when it comes to referring customers to you?

Eric: I am willing to give people free stuff, and I thank every person who referred us for business. I also congratulate the winners. If they get their calls answered and all of these extra touches, they love referring me.

IPS: Our next question is from David.

David: I appreciate the advice about using different fonts, and that will really help my newsletter.

Eric: I also use 'Jerry's Handwriting.' I have the worst handwriting, so I have now adopted this handwriting as the official handwriting of the agency.

David: My main question is about the "The Rule of 46™." Can you tell me about the transformation?

Eric: It was tough because the first biggest hurdle is trusting that other people are going to do what you do and do it well. What I have learned is that as I have surrounded myself with better, higher quality employees, they actually do stuff a lot better than I would have done it. Things get done more quickly and more efficiently. I have now created an office out of my home, so I do not even have to come in and get distracted, and I think it is important to be able to have private time. I find that, if I just try to sit in my office and try to work on the business, the staff still distracts me. I now spend more time working in my home office. It has been absolutely huge. My brother is envious because he has not pushed all of these principles to his own life yet, and so he is still working in the business. I am not, and we are bringing in more revenue.

IPS: Okay great, and our next question is from Brad.

Brad: What is the website that you use for the handwriting for your niece?

Eric: I use Dafont.com. You can download thousands of different fonts free, and they even give you systematic instructions.

Brad: Using your niece is a great idea!

Eric: I wanted to throw something in here: Michael has talked about being an insurance guru, and I am finding that I am now becoming one of the most hated insurance guys in Tampa, Florida. Agents and their wives are calling me saying how upset they are that I am taking business from them. With State Farm doing what it is doing, it has been a blessing for me, because customers are now shopping for the first time, and we have worked very hard to capitalize on it. Get Michael's box set on "How to be an Insurance Guru."

IPS: And here's Dave with our last question.

Dave: Can you review the way you do recordings?

Eric: I know Quantum Club™ offers a system, VidBiscuit™, for doing this that is just like mine but a lot easier for sending video emails to your customers and prospects. With my method, you have to have a fair amount of tech savvy and have a lot of different things set up. IPS's is plug-and-play, so it is very easy. It is very slick and very cool.

Dave: You send the video email with a video attached to the prospects along with the 28 reasons?

"Discover how VidBiscuit™, this new, super-easy "Video Email" service will catapult you to the top of the inbox, help you close more deals, cross-sell more customers, and lock in clients forever..."

Eric: Yes. The 28 reasons go via mail, because I am trying to hit them with different means, but I can attach things with the video email, so to the video email I attach the quote itself. Right now I have been piloting this myself, so I have been sending a generic email to the customer that says, "Thank you so much for calling, and I just want to tell you a little bit about our agency." It is kind of generic, but it is really working well. I am now going to get cameras for my salespeople. All of our customer service people are now using video cameras to talk to our customers doing care reviews face-to-face without our customers having to come in. You can use VidBiscuit™ and it's live. The CSR's send an email over to a customer and they can click on the video. All of a sudden, they can see my customer service rep. and we go through the care reviews and stuff like that right then. VidBiscuit™.com.

IPS: Eric, thanks very much for all of the contributions you have made to the IPS family.

Eric: My pleasure. Anybody who is coming out to Chicago, I would be happy to meet with you and talk if you would like to talk some more. If you have not signed up, I would suggest that you do. I have not missed a meeting. I am going to Chicago this week, and I already have my flights for Boston this next time out. It is extremely valuable; I would be happy to meet with and talk to anybody and show you my internal website.

"Michael's approach to marketing has "energized" me. I can't wait to get started on our new marketing program."
~David Joyce, Pittston, PA

"Michael, even though I still have not started any marketing campaign yet, joining Quantum Club has been a great eye opener for me- to know that everything that I'm doing wrong, and changes that I have to make starting with myself. This has been the best thing and the smartest thing I have done for myself and my business."
~Alice Shamoon, Sherman Oaks, CA

Glenn Agoncillo: Personal lines in California

Glenn Agoncillo, a budding city politician and local leader in Long Beach, California, joined Quantum Club™ in 2007 and is now a Principal at a $40 million agency. Originally hired as a personal lines manager in 2006, he worked his way up using Quantum Club™ techniques and in 2008 became a partner. Glenn's agency had an average of about 1.25 policies per client. He knew they could do better, and set about making the necessary changes. As a young man entering the industry, he knew he needed to demonstrate his worth and dedicate himself to improving the business that is his future, so he set ambitious goals for himself. His agency's client list has jumped to 2,352, an increase of nearly 500 in a year. Even more impressive, their number of total policies reached 7,544, an incredible leap of over 5,000 policies from the previous year!

IPS: *Glenn, you have done some incredible things with your agency, so let's take a look at the changes you've made and how you achieved such mind-boggling growth in both number of clients and number of policies. How many policies did you have a year ago and how many do you have now? How many customers?*

Glenn Agoncillo: After I did the Personal Lines Super Conference, we had 1,854 clients, and we had 2,314 total policies enforced, so that is averaging about 1.25 policies per client. We have always known that there was something wrong with that—the agency has been just cruising along. The Agency Principals were just okay with it, but I always thought we could do something different. Personal lines are pretty much the bread and butter of our agency, and they have been stable, but I knew that we could do more. And after doing the Personal Lines Super Conference and meeting other Quantum Club™ members, I had high goals for myself. I knew that in order to become an agency owner, I had to prove my worth. At the same time, I am in this for the long run. I have more at stake simply because I am a young guy, and I will be in this industry for a long time—so I knew I needed to set high goals for myself. As of right now, year to date we have 2,352 clients, so we grew by about 500 clients in a little over a year. And as far as total policies—this part is amazing—we are up to 7,544.

CROSS SELL

IPS: *So just to emphasize these numbers again: your client list grew by about 500. And you had 2,314 policies and you now have 7,544 policies, which mean you increased your policies by about 5,000! Clearly, you were using some impressive cross-sell strategies.*

Glenn: Definitely. Before I started working here, they thought that writing a mono-line auto was a client, but after I joined Quantum Club™, we redefined what the word 'client' meant to us.

IPS: *How do you define a client now?*

Glenn: A client must have a minimum of three policies with us. So for example, each client would have the auto policy, a homeowners or renters policy, and an umbrella policy—which is especially important in tough economic times. And when you sell people this protection, they will understand that, "Hey, you know what? This guy, this agency is really looking out for my best interest."

> "It is amazing how using principles of accountability, time management and delegating and creating the systems that make our day to day processes run more smoothly, can allow fewer people to do the same job, and actually does it better. I mean, these CSR's, they are just, amazing human beings."

IPS: *What else beyond the home or rental, auto and umbrella, what else does your department offer to these clients?*

Glenn: We also insure health, and we cross-sell, we transfer them to our life department, and if we find out that they own a business, then we cross-sell them or refer them to our commercial lines department.

IPS: *And how many CSR's are operating in your department?*

Glenn: Well, this is another crazy story I have to tell you. When I joined Quantum Club™ I had four full time CSR's and the only thing they did was make policy changes, talk to clients, and pretty much they were order-takers. And I had one policy specialist who would push paper, process the renewals and any memos that we received from the insurance companies. So with the policy specialist and the four CSR's, that would make it five, plus one salesperson and myself, for a total of seven. In the past year, I have actually downsized to two full-time CSR's, the quality specialist, and a full time personal lines sales agent. It is amazing how using principles of accountability, time management and delegating and creating the systems that make our day to day processes run more smoothly, can allow fewer people to do the same job, and actually do it better. I mean, these CSR's, they are just amazing human beings. Now, when I go to work, it's fun! This is a complete turnaround from where I was. Now I enjoy going to work, everything is just functioning how it is supposed to. Now even the commercial lines department can see what is going on in personal lines, and they want to be a part of it. They feel kind of neglected in comparison, and it is creating a hunger in that department to be part of what we are doing in personal lines.

IPS: *And of the 6 other people that were in that department when you joined Quantum Club™, how many of those people are still there?*

Glenn: Every single one is gone.

IPS: *And why are they gone?*

Glenn: Well, after joining Quantum Club™, I knew that I had to get with a team that would buy the vision, and the four CSR's that were there when I started just wouldn't buy the vision. They wouldn't buy that I knew the best direction for the agency.

IPS: *They were there before you got there, so they were really used to the way things were. It was comfortable for them, because it was the way they'd always done it. And you came in saying, 'This is the way we are going to do it". And they didn't want to buy into that?*

> "Another Quantum Club tool, ZipDrip™, has also helped us enormously. I tell you, it is insane! It is one of the greatest things that we've ever done!"

Glenn: They didn't want to buy into it at all.

IPS: *Alright, so you showed them the door. And as for the people that work for you now, what criteria were important to you in selecting and hiring those people?*

Glenn: First thing that I look for is personality. Everyone here in Long Beach knows who I am because I am very involved in the community, and our agency has been around for over 80 years, so we have a big, strong clientele of loyal clients. Everybody knows who I am, and that community involvement is an important part of our image. So my main criteria for hiring is personality, because you can't teach someone to be friendly or well-liked in the community, but you can teach them how to use the computer and you can teach them how to do paper work and process day-to-day stuff.

IPS: *Do they have experience in the industry before they come to you?*

Glenn: No.

IPS: *That is not important to you?*

Glenn: Nope. It was not important to me at all.

IPS: *Alright, so let's get back to the numbers that we heard before. How did you go from 2,300 to about 7,500 policies in such a short period of time?*

Glenn: We really, really, really, pushed on the cross-sell.

IPS: *Let's break that down—did CSR's push the cross- sale on inbound calls?*

ZIPDRIP™

Glenn: Yes, on inbound calls. We also did a mailing campaign; Claudia McClain, another Quantum Club™ member shared her letter with us, and we've customized that to our agency and to the environment here in southern California, and we've received tremendous responses from that. Another Quantum Club™ tool, ZipDrip™, has also helped us enormously. I tell you, it is insane! It is one of the greatest things that we've ever done.

IPS: *Can we talk a little bit about what ZipDrip™ is and how it has helped you? So in the personal lines department, let us say now you have about 2,300 or 2,400 clients. How many of their e-mail addresses do you have?*

Glenn: Let's see…we have close to about 2,000 now.

IPS: *That's good! Every so often, I'll ask for a show of hands at an event for the percentage of clients' e-mail addresses an agency has. Most of the hands start going down around 50%. Over the last few years I've noticed that more and more agents are realizing that the ZipDrip™ robot can do the work of getting e-mail addresses for you. Now many agencies have raised their percentages by about 10% to 20%. But Glenn, you've raised that number to 80% or so. That is pretty solid, and now you can reach a large majority of your clients easily by e-mail. So with ZipDrip™, besides the prewritten messages, do you write messages?*

Glenn: I do. I listened to one of Michael's WealthBuilder™ interviews, and I fully agree with him as far as the importance of personalizing your messages. And, like I said, everyone knows me here in Long Beach. They know who I am; they know my personality, so I make sure that when I send out those e-mails they hear my voice. And the same goes for my team; when clients call here, I want them to hear Glenn's message being delivered through Roger or through Sandra or through Scott or myself.

IPS: *Okay. Now let's talk about the inbound call and cross-sells. Are the CSR's incentivized?*

INCENTIVE PROGRAMS

Glenn: Yes. You have to incentivize them. You have to reward them. I try to change it up a bit. First I started using the Prize Wheel to give out rewards. And I actually ask my team to put the rewards that they want on the wheel.

IPS: Oh, that is brilliant!

Glenn: I figured I shouldn't come up with the rewards because it is their prize, so I let them choose.

IPS: So what are the kinds of things on your wheel?

Glenn: Let's see. A full spa day, cash, oh and here is the kicker…gets paid for ½ day. That's what they all wanted. They were afraid to ask, but I said, "Hey, just ask me…I mean, I will be more than happy to put it in there just as long as you guys show me the numbers."

IPS: Alright, do you remember where you got the wheel?

Glenn: I got it from the web site.

IPS: So if somebody goes to the search-bar, they just type in Prize Wheel.

Glenn: Yep.

IPS: Prize Wheel, okay. And if somebody can't do it, call our office because we have one too and we can help you find it. So how do they earn points for this spin?

Glenn: They earn points with the number of cross-sells that they make. First, to keep it realistic and just to get them into the groove of things, I said that five cross-sells earn them a poker chip, and for every three poker chips they have, they can spin the wheel. The poker chip just adds a little more interest and excitement. And as soon as they start getting programmed and used to the routine, then they said, "Five is easy! I can do ten!" So then I said that if they did more cross-sells, I would bump up the rewards. I mean, they deserve it. So now it's more like 10 poker chips for a spin, but I've also doubled the prizes, so instead of a paid ½ day, the reward is a paid full day.

IPS: *So when do you spin the wheel?*

Glenn: We spin at the end of each month, and everyone hears it. Even the commercial department hears it…

IPS: *You are driving those guys crazy.*

Glenn: We are! You know what? It has been a tough 6 months, but I have to tell you; they are starting to get into the groove of what personal is doing, which is great.

"Cross Selling: fastest, cheapest way to grow your book of business."

IPS: *Okay. I can't remember how many slots are on the wheel.*

Glenn: There are twenty-four.

IPS: *And so somewhere on there is the spa day, the paid day, and some cash, and whatever other prizes they might choose.*

Glenn: Yep, I change it up based on what they want.

IPS: *Alright. Now another question, is there any form of public accountability? For example, does everybody know how many cross-sells each employee makes?*

Glenn: Yes. We announce everything at the end of the month and, you know, at first when I tried it with the original CSR's, they were weirded out by the whole thing.

IPS: *They probably hated you.*

Glenn: Yeah, they did. They really did. I was the most hated person here in the office.

IPS: *Well, all too often, that is what happens. Everyone wants to prove to you that the numbers are not going to go up, that what you're doing won't work, and that creates this sort of gang mentality. They all want to show this new guy that you can't cross that one in this marketplace or whatever the latest excuse is. But I guess the new team has shown them otherwise.*

Glenn: Definitely.

IPS: *Alright. And do you get a lot of responses from your mailings?*

Glenn: We get a lot of responses from the mail, and we also get a lot of responses from my personalized ZipDrip™ message. As far as the mail, we have just some little return slips that say, "Hey! Contact this person or contact me," and they have all of my account managers' information on them. When we send out mailings, we split up our client list alphabetically, and so every mail that goes out shows my account managers' names and my CSRs names and that way the clients contact them directly instead of contacting me. And we get a huge response off of that. It used to have my name, but now I actually miss my name on the letters, because it's not on them anymore!

REFERRAL PROGRAM

IPS: *What are you doing for referral's right now?*

Glenn: We give them two options for a reward. They can either get a gift card from us with a note saying, "Hey! By the way…thanks for the referral." Or they also have the option to donate it to a local charity of their choice. So, those are the two options that we have for referrals.

IPS: *Okay. And do you do any big thing at the end of the year? Or is it just one at a time?*

ENGAGEMENT

Glenn: Just one at a time but we also do something else to foster strong client relationships. In our newsletters, we have this contest called "Garden of the Month."
A lot of our clients e-mail us pictures of their gardens, and we send them out in the newsletter. The next month, clients vote on which is the best one. We don't vote on it—we want our clients to vote on it simply because it makes interaction a little different.

IPS: *That's beautiful. So how many pictures do you put in to be voted on?*

Glenn: We receive about twenty-five photos. You know, I try to make it fun for everyone. We have fun here, but we also make it fun for our clients.

IPS: *So what does a client get if they win "Garden of the Month?"*

> "I am just trying to encourage my clients to keep up their gardens! Keep up their houses! Lower loss ratios, lower or fewer claims...."

Glenn: Oh! We give them a fifty-dollar gift certificate to Home Depot or Lowes or another home and garden store. I am just trying to encourage my clients to keep up their gardens! Keep up their houses! Lower loss ratios, lower or fewer claims...we are just trying to get them into the groove of making sure that their house is always in tip-top condition.

IPS: *Well, that's unusual and very clever. Now, your newsletter is going out every month?*

Glenn: Yes

IPS: *And it is going out to all of your clients? Does it go out to your commercial lines department clients?*

Glenn: Yes. We are starting to try to involve commercial. Our commercial lines are kind of unique because we do a lot of out of state business, we have a lot of railroad insurance throughout the United States, and so we have to customize our newsletters to them as well. I am trying to get the other partners here at the agency to help out and make them accountable. I am more than happy to share my ideas, but it is up to them to create the newsletter for the commercial clients because I can't do everything by myself. The fact is that they are seeing the results in personal lines, and they want to achieve those same results.

IPS: *Okay...good. Are there any other unusual aspects of your newsletter?*

Glenn: <u>Newsletters,</u> no. <u>Keep them plain and simple.</u> I mean, here in Southern California, everybody is on the go, so I just try to keep it plain and simple with brief messages at the top and lots of pictures. Colorful, and little tips here and there and also reminding everyone that we are a full service agency and about our referral program and everything else. I also have pictures of my account mangers there too, so that way the clients who are out of the state or in Northern California, or outside Long Beach or Los Angeles County, can still get to know who they are talking to.

IPS: *And how is your retention rate now?*

Glenn: It has improved. When I first started working here in 2006, it was at 85%. When I first joined Quantum Club™, it was in the high 80's, and now, we are at about 92.7%. I know we can get it higher.

IPS: *Well, you probably can, but to go from 85% to almost 93% well, pull up the Easy Millions™ spreadsheet on a* book as big as yours, and you will see that over a ten-year period, that is already a lot of money.

Glenn: I'll never forget my trip to Minneapolis because that was when I saw the numbers and how much money we could be making off of cross-selling and retention. After that I worked my butt off just trying to create a system to get that going. I really understood how much money we were losing just by not increasing our retention by even one percentage point. So seeing those numbers on the Easy Millions™ spreadsheet really made a huge impact on developing this system.

IPS: Well, I can't encourage our members enough…I really think people should spend more time with our spreadsheets, and they should, at a minimum, annually do the Easy Millions™ spreadsheet, the Cross-Sell spreadsheet, and the Three Dimensional Growth™ Program spreadsheet. I mean, for pretty much every single aspect of an agency, we figured a way to display the numbers so you can look at it from a new point of view. Then you can sit down with key members of the team and share with them how much value and strength they can bring to the agency if they just do a few simple things, like cross-sell and

> "A year and a half ago, I would never think of the business as fun, but now I am having fun! I am actually looking forward to the next twenty-five, thirty years that are ahead of me. I am really excited to find out what is going to happen!"

increase retention. Okay, so you've also done some other things, like clarifying internal processes in your agency. And are things running more smoothly than they were before?

Glenn: A lot more!

IPS: *And you've got over 5,000 more policies than when you started. And you've got a smaller team.*

Glenn: We do have a smaller team than before. When I used to have four full time CSR's and two of them were out sick, everyone was just running around here with their heads chopped off, but now if I have one CSR out, the system is in place to take care of it. And of course, if you have more policy counts per client, each person does less work. And if you obtain the right kind of business that works for your agency, you rarely get any phone calls for crazy things or little billing questions, which mean the CSR's can be using their time doing more important things.

> "…everyone in Quantum Club™ is generous and creative and…just ask for help, because they will help you."

IPS: *And you use processes that people understand, routine ways that you do business? And this method produces predictable results?*

Glenn: Yes.

IPS: *So obviously, we are very strong advocates of that...Glenn is there anything else that you want us to pass on?*

Glenn: You know when they brought me here, I did have a great foundation, but after joining Quantum Club™, I had to do some retro fitting. The industry changes, and so does everyone else. One of the most important things is to have a team that is really accountable. And I tell you, this whole thing has been kind of like an evolution or a rebirth for me. A year and a half ago, I would never think of the business as fun, but now I am having fun! I am actually looking forward to the next twenty-five, thirty years that are ahead of me. I am really excited to find out what is going to happen.

IPS: *Yeah, the marketplace had better get ready for you! I had mentioned to you earlier that when I met you I knew, after seeing your reaction the first day, this guy is on fire! He is going to get some things done. I think it is an inspiration, Glenn, for a lot of people because for us to say "a year from now, eighteen months from now, can the change really be that dramatic?" Well, you've proven it can, so, congratulations!*

Glenn: Thank you, Thank you. Thank you to your team, and everyone else at Quantum Club™.

IPS: *Well, yes! There are a whole lot of aspects to Quantum Club™. I think probably our greatest strength is the sharing and the generosity, so I want to thank you for sharing as well.*

Glenn: Yeah I'd love to share some advice about that. When it comes to new members, I know what it felt like when I was a new member. I know that there are times when you feel like, "I don't know how this person is going to respond" or, "I don't know if this person is going to e-mail me back with tips," but just ask questions, and don't be afraid. You'll be surprised. I mean, everyone in Quantum Club™ is generous and creative and…just ask for help, because they will help you.

IPS: *Good advice, Glenn. And I want to congratulate you on your success. I am very, very impressed, and I think you've done a marvelous job there. And I know that people have questions. I am sure they can contact you, but you are also one of those guys who show up. We tend to see you at events so I will pass that on as advice to everyone. One of the things we find as the common denominator among those who really get things done, really use new strategies and succeed is that they tend to show up. And, if you do, you'll probably run into Glenn. Glenn, thank you so much for your generosity in sharing.*

"Using the principles we learned from Michael, we put together a marketing campaign that, frankly, has the rest of the agency in awe. We've added $1.86 million in premium in the first six months of the program. At the rate we're going, I expect this to be a $4,000,000.00 program by the end of the year!"
~Marty Burger, Stratford, CT

"Being able to listen and extract valuable information from some of the continent's best insurance agents lets you move on with confidence that you can dominate the insurance marketing in your region or niche!"
-Terry O'Connor, Charlotte, NC

Gordon Sorrel and Leigh Ann Johnson: Commercial and Personal lines from Texas

Gordon Sorrel, has been in the industry since 1977 and is the Principal of Texas Insurance and Financial Services in El Campo, Texas. He has been a member of Quantum Club™ since 2005. In 1996, his agency realized the advantages of niche marketing and they have since become masters at it. Leigh Ann Johnson, the marketing genius behind Texas Insurance and Financial Services, has played an integral role in the agency's success as well—so integral that when Gordon won the Best of the Best Contest, he gave the prize (a Porsche) to Leigh Ann. They focus largely on commercial business, but have some personal lines clients as well. Gordon and Leigh Ann's experience clearly shows that even if you have many years of experience in the industry, Quantum Club™ can still offer new systems and strategies to help your agency grow and evolve.

IPS: Hello! I hope everybody is having a terrific day. I have a couple of my favorite people on the line. First we have Gordon Sorrel, the winner of our Best of the Best Contest from the recent Summit, and second, one of the people he gives credit to for making his agency as successful as it is, Leigh Ann Johnson. Gordon and Leigh Ann from Texas Insurance and Financial Services—how are you guys?

Gordon Sorrel: We are here and ready to go!

IPS: We have a lot of ground to cover, and I know that everyone is excited to hear about what you have done in the last few years to become as successful as you have been. Let us begin with a little bit of a basic background. Gordon, I will first turn to you. How did you get in the industry, and how long have you been doing it? Tell us a little bit about what the agency does.

Gordon: I got into the industry many moons ago, back in the late seventies, when I was involved in property management and was trying to figure out a way to even out my income. It seemed like it was chicken-and-feathers, so I decided that I wanted a more steady income, and I figured that insurance would be a great way to even out my income flow. Then I found out pretty quickly that it was my first love, so I sold everything else and focused on insurance. We Incorporated in 1982, and shortly after that moved from the Houston market into El Campo, Texas figuring that I could do anything I did not used to do in Houston. That is the decision I made, and it was not too long after that Leigh Ann joined us and we started doing some very good things. Leigh Ann had a lot of energy and was focused on marketing, and we fell upon some niche markets that were very productive for us. They were so productive that we decided we would expand it and get into some other areas.

IPS: *How many people are there on your team now, Gordon?*

Gordon: Right now we have a total of sixteen staff members and six producers.

IPS: *Roughly, you are split between commercial, personal, and other lines of business?*

Gordon: Yes. We do about ninety-percent commercial and ten-percent personal lines. A large section of our commercial business is crop insurance, so we do about $7 million in crop insurance, and we do about $7 million plus in commercial, and close to $3 million in personal lines.

IPS: *Leigh Ann, what is the role that you play in the agency?*

Leigh Ann Johnson: The Jackie of All Trades! Actually, marketing is my main focus now. When I started with the agency I was doing accounting, office management, marketing, IT…a little bit of everything. As the agency grew, it was important for me to focus on what I do best, and we determined that was marketing, so that is my main focus. I do, however, work with the ladies in the office on implementing new procedures and am the backup when they need it. I do whatever needs to be done here at the agency.

IPS: *Let us talk about what you have done to make your agency grow as much as you have. You have been a member of Quantum Club™, Gordon, since '05. One other* *question I wanted to ask you: how many States are you licensed in?*

Gordon: We are licensed in thirty-five States.

IPS: *If you are going to look at the big ideas or big strategies you have had that have made your agency successful, what comes to mind?*

Gordon: Without a doubt it is niche marketing.

IPS: *I have a list of about six different associations that you have affiliations with. How do you go about selecting your niches, and what are your criteria for niche selection?*

> **Criteria for Niche Marketing:**
> "The first criteria is being good at writing that niche. The second is having markets that write that niche. The third is having sales people that can focus in that niche."

Gordon: The first criteria is being good at writing that niche. The second is having markets that write that niche. The third is having sales people that can focus in that niche. Once those are answered affirmatively, the next step is spending enough time immersed in that niche so we can actually speak the language of the industry to the people that are in that industry. Every industry has its own language.

IPS: *They do! And when I look at your list of niches, they are pretty diverse. Your agency needs to learn a lot of languages.*

Gordon: Yes, and that is where the sales people come in.

IPS: *For example, you have the American Bee Keeping Federation, so you have bee keepers. You also have the Head Start Association and the Texas Association of Community Action Agencies, and that is not bee keeping. You have three Nursery Associations and a Landscaping Association. You have Oil, and Gas. You have really considerable diversity in your niche penetration, and you have a mark of dominance in some of these.*

Gordon: We do. In three of those niches, we have received endorsements from the associations and, once you get an endorsement from an Association, from that point forward it is a slam-dunk. Everybody wants to deal with the expert. For example, the people who own the Wholesale Nurseries we write for do not understand that we do other things, and they really do not care. As far as they are concerned, the only thing we write is their business, and that is fine with us. We try to propagate that myth. The bottom-line is that we want them to look to us as the experts in the industry.

IPS: *Let us take one of these as an example and walk through how you have cultivated the relationship, and how you take full advantage of the relationship with the Bee Keepers Association. I would say that the average agency would not want to write bee keepers. First of all, they are going to have to figure out and hunt down a market for them, and the premiums are likely not significant in many cases. Is that true?*

Gordon: We want to be the expert to the degree that we can write the professional, the guy who is harvesting gallons of honey, if not drums of honey, for a living. That is where the real money is. The big dollars in commercial insurance is with those people. We have to start somewhere, so that is where the endorsement with the association comes in. What we find out is that a lot of the large, successful enterprises sit on these Boards of Directors regardless of whatever niche you are talking about. The people you really want to zero-in on are the people who sit on the Board of Directors of that Trade Associations. As a general rule, they are not the 'mom and pops,' they are the guys who are doing extremely well in their industry.

IPS: How did you get from being a "Main Street" agency in El Campo, Texas to securing an official endorsement with the American Bee Keeping Federation?

> "We want to be the expert to the degree that we can write the professional, the guy who is harvesting gallons of honey, if not drums of honey, for a living. That is where the real money is. The big dollars in commercial insurance is with those people."

ASSOCIATION ENDORSEMENTS

Gordon: We had a bee keeper here in El Campo and, as it turns out, he was President of the Texas Association of Bee Keepers. He came into the office one day and said his insurance was being canceled. He showed me his policy and it was written by an agent in North Dakota. I asked him why he felt like he had to go to North Dakota to get insurance, and he explained that these people were the experts in the industry. The light bulb went off in my head right there! We got to talking about his industry and, like any man who has a great deal of pride in his work, you start asking about his business and how he accomplished what he accomplished, and he could talk for hours. He told us that he was President of the Texas Association of Bee Keepers and was very active in the Association. He was disappointed that this particular agent was dropping him because they did not want to write certain coverage's that he felt he needed. I explained that I would do my homework and be in touch. I got a real education during our two-hours of conversation, and that was probably the best two-hours of conversation I have ever spent. We found out that there was some real pain in that arena. Once we did that, we figured out how to solve the pain by calling around and finding out that there is some natural hesitancy in underwriters when writing that class of business, even though they had no actual data to support their fears. It just sounded like a class of business they did not want to write and that just was not good enough. We went to the Texas Department of Insurance and started gathering some actual data. We found out that it is an extremely clean class of business with virtually no losses in it! Armed with that data in hand from the Texas Department of Insurance, we marched into the regional office of an insurance company in San Antonio and explained that we thought we could make some money doing this. They looked at the numbers, saw the data, and wanted to take a second look because they may have prejudiced it based on their own natural fears. Our attitude was if our company is doing it then every other company is doing it, too. That clears the field; therefore, if I can convince my companies to do it, there is no one to compete with. That is basically what we did; we got some companies on board and started writing some business.

IPS: *How did you get your first customers?*

Gordon: It <u>started with referrals from the client</u> I wrote here in El Campo. Because of his connections with the Texas Association of Bee Keepers, he started referring me to head-honchos in the association. From there I found out that they have Association meetings, which I started to attend. They suggested to me that I give talks on insurance. That provided a tremendous amount of credibility because I was introduced by the President of the Association. Then we joined as an affiliated industry to their business, and one thing led to another. We started asking questions about endorsements, which they had given unsuccessfully in the past because no one was willing to work. We made a commitment to them, a commitment that makes you wonder if you are smart in doing this, and the commitment was if they give us the endorsement, we will make a promise that we will get licensed in any State where there is a bee keeper that wants our business. We knew the licensing fees in some States are pretty steep, so we did not know if we would make any money doing that. What they did not know is that we had other niches, such as our Wholesale Nurseries, so we could work hand-in-glove in those States. <u>Once you get a license, you can write anything in that State.</u> It does not have to be limited to bee keepers. It opened other doors for us and allowed us to move in to some other areas.

IPS: *So you have really become a National Insurance Agency?*

Gordon: We have, and we did it with an office in El Campo, Texas. We have an 800-number and a website. Leigh Ann does a phenomenal job of developing landing pages for each one of our niches.

IPS: You have a half-dozen or so landing pages or sites for your niches?

Gordon: Oh yes! She can tell you about that. She does a great job with that, and it displays us to the insurance-buying public as the experts they are looking for. That is what we want our advertising to say to the public.

IPS: With the Bee Keepers Association and with the others, what do they do for you? Do they give you the mailing list? Do they include mailers from you in their mailings? How do they give you access?

> "…it displays us to the insurance-buying public as the experts they are looking for. That is what we want our advertising to say to the public."

Gordon: They do both. We ship boxes of brochures to the American Bee Keepers Federation, which is located in Jessop, GA, every two to three months. They pass these brochures out because they are getting constant inquiries, from bee keepers across the Nation, about an insurance agent that can help them out. They mail out our brochures for us. In addition to that, as a member of the Association, we have access to all of the other members of the Association through a mailing list. That is the key to joining the Association: you immediately become a member, and members want to talk to members, and every Association wants to promote members talking to members; therefore, they give you the mailing list which includes email addresses, snail-mail addresses, and websites. It gives you a tremendous amount of access across-the-board to a client base that has one thing in common: they want the product that you have.

IPS: *Are you active in their conferences and trade-shows and things like that?*

Gordon: Absolutely! We do everything we can to <u>immerse ourselves in that industry</u>. We have one trade-show that has an 'Eat and Greet.' During their conference they have a break area, and we sponsor that; we buy the donuts and coffee for that and post a sign that says 'Texas Insurance' or 'Bee Keeping Insurance Specialists' or 'Wholesale Nursery Specialists,' depending on which show we are at. We get a lot of advertising from that because people get tired at these shows and look for a break area, or they want to talk business away from their shop so they go to the break area to get a cup of coffee and donut. This is where they see our sponsorship.

IPS: *Leigh Ann, what would you add to this conversation?*

TRADE SHOWS

Leigh Ann: There are so many different aspects that have to be considered when putting a trade-show together, from the trade-show program to the trade magazine that follows. Sponsorship of an event begins with ZipDrip™, a postcard, or a pre-mailer that goes out prior to a show.

IPS: *Let us talk about that for a second. Do you get the registration list prior to a show?*

Leigh Ann: Actually, we send it out to the member list.

IPS: *You send it out to everybody? So prior to the show, you tell them to come by the booth.*

Leigh Ann: Yes. We tell them to come by the booth and briefly explain the products we have to offer. Back in November, we had a bee keeping show in Tyler, Texas and we ordered some really cool four-ounce honey bottles; we filled the honey bottles with a little note about Texas Insurance.

IPS: *Do you capture lead information at the trade-show?*

Leigh Ann: Yes, we do. Typically we will have a giveaway item at the booth. Years ago, we started it at one or two shows and when we stopped. We got negative feedback about why we did not have it. This sounds a little corny but it works. We have a jar at the booth and it has a 'guess the number.' At a bee keeper show, we might have the jar stocked with Bit-O-Honey and a one-hundred-dollar bill in it. Someone guesses the correct number and wins the Bit-O-Honey and the money. We do that at every show and it is a huge hit. People come by our booth year-after-year.

IPS: *So they have to give you their business card or fill something out. And after the show, how do you follow up with them?*

Leigh Ann: Postcards, ZipDrip™, phone calls, photo note cards… You name it!

IPS: Anything else on niche marketing?

Gordon: The key is to keep in contact with your clients and prospect base. Leigh Ann's rule is that we want to touch base with every prospect in that Association once per month. Postcards are a cheap and easy way to do it. ZipDrip™ for e-mails has worked very well, also. Once every six-months, we may come out with a lump e-mail to contact them, but the bottom line is that we keep our name in front of them. We have a very simple slogan: Insurance Simplified. Everyone that calls us thinks that insurance is so complex and they do not know what to do, so we came up with 'Insurance Simplified,' and we make it as simple as we can. That is what we do.

IPS: By the way, if Quantum Club™ members have questions for Gordon or Leigh Ann, please write them down for when we open up the lines. Before we do that, there are two or three other things that I think we need to cover, because niche marketing is only one of your success secrets. You added, according to our records from the contest, 1,047 new policies this year. How did you do that?

> "Leigh Ann's rule is that we want to touch base with every prospect in that Association once per month."

REFERRAL PROGRAM

Gordon: A big chunk of that was our referral program. We give away $1,000 in American Express gift cards to a lucky client, and we get our producers involved in that, too.

Their client base is a good source of referrals in addition to the existing client base that is already there.

IPS: *You do that at the end of the year?*

Gordon: Our little community here has a parade every year, and we capitalize on that. We have people stacked up in front of our office to watch the parade, and we hand out food and have a drawing. We give away $1,000 at that parade. We draw a lot of attention to ourselves. People are excited about it. In everything we do, we try to project a positive image of ourselves.

IPS: *How do you tie the referral program into the parade?*

Leigh Ann: In November we send out the calendars for the year; in the calendar, we put an invite to our Christmas Open-House announcing the Referral winner. That goes out to clients. We put an ad in the newspaper for two or three weeks prior to the parade. This year, Gordon and I happened to be in the parade. It was really cool that out of the entire parade route, our block was stacked about twenty-people deep. It was great.

Gordon: A friend of mine had a 1934 Ford and drove so we could ride. We put our magnetic signs on the side of the car and rode the parade from one end of the route to the other.

IPS: *And how does someone qualify for the referral contest?*

Gordon: The referral contest we have is a means by which we have clients and prospects refer other prospects to us. The way we do that is very simple: if you refer someone to us, you get an immediate gift of two lottery tickets, a 'thank you' card, and enrollment into our monthly drawing of a forty-dollar gift card to be used at a restaurant of your choice in our community. The annual prize we give away is $1,000. So, there are three ways you can win and it is something that we do every year, so we have our client base trained to give us the names of their friends and neighbors.

IPS: *Any idea how many referrals you got last year?*

Leigh Ann: I think it was 253.

IPS: *Do you know your closing ratio on those?*

Gordon: It was not as good as we wanted it to be. I think it was 65%.

IPS: *Still, that gave you 25% of your additional policies for the year.*

COMMUNITY INVOLVEMENT

Gordon: Exactly, and that is a big chunk of it right there. We do a lot of things and really get involved in our community. We have a producer in our office who is President of Boys and Girls Club in El Campo. Another producer is involved with Knights of Columbus. All of our producers are involved in civic and community activities.

IPS: *I see a list of about 12 things you are active in within your community: the Ricebird Booster Club, the Boys and Girls Club, the Knights of Columbus, the County Youth Fair, the Dairy Merit Heifer Sponsorship, the El Campo Memorial Hospital Soup Cook-off, the Wharton County*

Community Foundation, the Lions Club Rotary Sponsor, St. Philip and St. Robert's Catholic Church Picnic Assistance, the Museum Board, and the Christmas Parade. You cannot turn around in El Campo without running into you guys, can you?

Gordon: That is the truth! We want our salespeople to understand that part of their job description is being involved in the community. If you are not putting something back into the community, we really do not want you in our agency. It makes it really simple.

IPS: Let's talk about your cross-selling campaigns and efforts. You significantly increased the number of policies per customer this past year.

CROSS SELLING

Gordon: Yes. When our clients call in or when our CSR's call a client with a question regarding renewal or an endorsement, it gives them an opportunity to ask about missing insurance coverage and/or information. We tell our staff that we are not asking them to sell; we are asking them to nurture. These people are like your children, and you would not allow your children to run outside without a coat or a hat, and we do not want our client base to run outside without the proper insurance. We are nurturing, not selling.

Leigh Ann: I would say that a big part of the turnaround for our agency came about two years ago when our entire CSR staff was part of the CSR Mastery Program™. It started where we really did not have the buy-in, but it became a competition within a month. If personal lines got ten client service report cards back then others in other departments wanted to get more than ten. As I walked around the office, I noticed that WOW experience every time." It became a mindset, even though they did not buy in at the beginning. By the end of the year, each one wanted to be the best. That really helped both the agency and the ladies.

IPS: *You have really knocked your retention out of the ballpark, and I am sure that the contact and communication between the CSR's and your customers and the marketplace is an important part of it, but let me take a look at these figures. Your commercial lines retention went from 87% to 94%, personal lines retention went from 85% to 95% percent, and your health and life retention went from 96% to 99%. My recollection is that your crop retention is at 100%. Those are good numbers!*

RETENTION

Gordon: Those are phenomenal numbers! I never will forget the first Closed Door Session I went to with Quantum Club™ back in the first year I joined. There was

IPS: What are some of the strategies that you implement throughout the year to increase your retention?

Gordon: We like to have 'exit strategies.' If a client is moving out of our agency, I want to know why. It better be a good reason.

IPS: And what have you discovered from that?

Gordon: We try to get better at what we are doing, and the only way to do that is to find out why people are leaving our agency. I cannot stress that enough.

> "I never will forget the first Closed Door Session I went to with Quantum Club…there was this guy who stood up, Lee Hendrie, and he said 'One of the things I have discovered in my agency is that for every 1% I can improve my retention, $300,000 drops to my bottom line.' I asked him later to tell me about that, and that kind of put us on fire."

CLIENT NURTURING

IPS: *What do you do to nurture your clients throughout the year?*

Leigh Ann: We send birthday and 'thank you' cards; we cut out newspaper articles and send them to the families. We do ZipDrip™. The list goes on and on. I have been marketing this way for so long that it does not even seem like marketing anymore. It is just a natural course of events.

Gordon: We had a phenomenal amount of success doing our newsletters; the problem was that we could not keep the newsletters going. That was a real bummer for me; I felt like it was something we should have kept going, but there seemed like there were a million reasons why we did not. I cannot say that enough: if anyone is out there who is even toying with the idea of newsletters, I am encouraging you to do it because it works extremely well. Rounding out the accounts significantly increases your retention.

IPS: *In personal lines, you have some kind of relationship with Real Estate Agents. Tell us how that works.*

Gordon: I have encouraged our sales staff to get involved with mortgage companies and real estate people. The key to writing that business is being at the point of sale, and that is where these people are. They are at the point of sale all of the time, so if you can cultivate some relationships there then obviously someone has to recommend an insurance agent to the new kid in town. In most cases, it is the realtor and they will hand them the Yellow Pages. I would just as soon have them referred to us, and not only in our community. We are about thirty-minutes down the road from a large portion of Houston, so we capitalize on that suburban area of Houston that is just down the road from us. We can issue policies here and get them to the closing table as quickly as any agency in Houston.

IPS: *Do you do anything on an ongoing basis to nurture the relationships you have with the Real Estate Agents who give you referrals?*

Gordon: We call them 'Routine Visits' and 'Shoe Leather.' You get out and visit these people and, every time, you give them something; it does not matter what it is, you just give them something like a notepad or a pen. You get to their office at least once per week and ask if they have anything for you; you also ask about themselves and their family to personalize it as much as you can. Showing people you care and that you are available is huge. I cannot mention anything that is bigger than those two elements.

IPS: One more thing I wanted to ask you both: who is driving the Porsche?

Leigh Ann: Me!

IPS*: Of all of the cars I have ever given away, I miss that one the most. I think the reason I wanted to raise that, Gordon, is so that you could say a word or two about that. You won a Porsche and handed the keys over to Leigh Ann.*

Gordon: Leigh Ann is the one who works extremely hard and takes care of the marketing in our office. I cannot say enough good things about Leigh Ann and what she has done with the marketing in our office. Leigh Ann has been with us about fifteen-years now, and we have averaged $1 million in new business every year since she has been here. As we have grown, what I have tried to do is strip away the jobs Leigh Ann has been doing that someone else can do better; that way it enables her to focus on the job she does best, and that has been a reward of growth. She gets to spend more and more time doing the thing she likes. Because of that, I felt it was very important for her to get the Porsche.

IPS: *That is true for all of us: the reward of growth is that we get to do more and more of what it is that we love.*

Gordon: It is, and it is called "specialization." Every agency needs to experience that, and if you are not experiencing that, then you are not growing. It is a reward.

IPS: *I think your agency also got ten-thousand-dollars to spread amongst your staff.*
In a smaller agency that ten-thousand-dollars can really mean a lot.

Leigh Ann: After a 19 hour trip home, that Monday morning we cut the checks and divided it out. It was really an awesome event.

IPS: *That is fantastic. What was the reaction? How did the team respond to that?*

Gordon: It was unanimous. After we won the $10,000, I asked them if they wanted it with their normal Christmas bonus or if they wanted it then. They wanted it right then. Our people, thanks to Quantum Club™, actually got two bonuses this year. They really earned it and it is very much appreciated.

IPS: *Building A Gifted Team™ has always been a high value for your agency. What are some of the things you do that stand out there?*

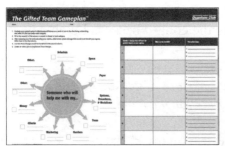

Gordon: One of the things I am excited about is that we have a group of gifted and talented people who believe in putting back into the community. The people in our community see our people in a job or a duty other than insurance. They see them working at the Youth Fair, at Knights of Columbus, at Boys and Girls Club, and at other endeavors in the community. The fact that we are here really cements the relationship with the community. I do not know that there is another agency in our town, and there are ten of them, that will do the things that we do in our community. I cannot tell you the dividends that it pays because what we do, we do very sincerely. We do it because we like this community, and I think the people in our town know that. I would encourage you, if you like the place that your living, to get involved in it and put something back in it instead of just taking from it. If you are sincere about that, you will find that the community will rally around you.

IPS: *One last thing before we open it up for questions. I have not replaced the Porsche, and normally I am* *replacing the car in October. I simply have not decided whether or not we are going to run the contest the same way next year. I am not going to think about it for a few weeks; if we do, however, run some kind of a contest next year, what would you say to people who are thinking about it?*

Gordon: I would say to them, "Remember this is a marketing organization and because it's a marketing organization, you better put your best marketing foot forward when you come to the contest because Leigh Ann is going to!

IPS: *Well said! While the operator is getting names, can you tell us what the bus trip is for the team?*

Leigh Ann: We took a bus trip on my birthday.

Gordon: We went on a Saturday and took spouses and significant others along, also.

Leigh Ann: We went to the nearest gambling establishment in Louisiana. We spent six or seven hours there. It was just a fun way to spend time with the people you work with and with their families outside of the office.

> "Our people, thanks to Quantum Club™ actually got two bonuses this year."

Gordon: It was a lot of fun. Everyone got a chance to spend a little money, have a little fun, and blow off some steam. We had a designated driver and it was a lot of fun, both going and coming. We did a little relationship building on the way there and back.

IPS: Do we have any questions? Hello Jerry!

Jerry: I wanted to say that for me, personally, Gordon and Leigh Ann have both been an inspiration and an encouragement to me and to other people in Quantum Club™, as well. I have a few questions for you. How many trade shows to you participate in per year and who works them?

Gordon: Probably six or seven per year. Coming up in January, I have a bee keepers meeting in Sacramento; I have another one coming up in Orlando, Florida and then one in Conroe, Texas just north of Houston. Those are three that are in January. We then have another in February up near Dallas, and then another in San Antonio in August. We are scattered out all over the country. In October we go to two or three more, so we are going to be at six or seven of them scattered throughout the year.

Jerry: My final question is this: my sister lives in Texas, so if I refer her, can I get in on the possibility to win one-thousand-bucks?

Gordon: Absolutely! You can even win one-million-dollars on the raffle tickets we send you!

IPS: Thanks Jerry. Our next caller is Larry. Hi, Larry!

Larry: Our agency, for the last ten years, has had a contractors niche that is, of course, suffering a bit because of everything going on in the construction world. We are trying to diversify and IPS has been helping me with that.

There is some resistance in our office to getting more involved in personal lines. I am curious – in your agency, do the same people who write commercial accounts also do personal lines? Or is there someone in the office you brought in just to do personal lines?

Gordon: We definitely segment the duties in our office. I do not want the people in our office who do commercial lines talking to people about personal lines other than to say, "Can I refer you to someone in that department?" That is all I want them to say. I do not want them to take a stab in the dark. We want to present ourselves to the insurance-buying public as professionals and as professionals you cannot wear more than one hat. If you are good in commercial, then stay in commercial. If you have different departments in your office then let each one approach a client from a team concept. Clients love the team concept; they appreciate the various area of expertise as opposed to the one guy who is trying to be all things to all people.

"Niches to Riches training will teach you how to get trade associations, professional societies and other organizations to support you, endorse you and market for you!"

IPS: Our next caller is Kevin.

Gordon: Hello Kevin! How are you doing?

Kevin: I am doing great! As Jerry said, you guys were truly an inspiration at the Summit. That was a great presentation. As you build out these niches, how much of your production comes from outside producers versus the CSR's in the office?

Gordon: That is a very good question! I would say that probably fifty-percent of our new business comes from outside producers; Leigh Ann is saying it is closer to seventy-five, and she may be right on that! The bottom line is that we do not depend on outside producers for 100%. I want my inside people to be involved in asking people for the business. I tell my producers that if my inside people get a piece of business that you feel like you should have gotten, then why didn't you call first?

IPS: Our next caller is Russ. Hi, Russ.

Russ: Good morning and congratulations you two. It is very well deserved. Gordon, I love your comment about being 'specialists' and about specializing. I definitely think that is our future in insurance. On your account rounding, are you doing anything besides the competition in the office? Is there other incentive for your employees? How are you promoting that rounding even more?

Gordon: We have a very convoluted bonus program that we use, and it works very well. Last year, we gave away $46,000 to our staff. It is very simple: we have a target, and that target is 25% growth in profitability and 25% growth in production. Those are quantifiable numbers because you know what your profit was last year, what your growth was last year, and what your bottom line was last year. We set aside $35,000 for production and $25,000 for profitability. If we hit 12.5% profitability, then they only get a percentage of that $25,000 for profitability, and the same is true for growth. We have four departments in our office: personal lines, commercial lines, crop insurance, and life and health. The top department in growth gets 35% of the totals, and then it is split down from there amongst the other departments. Profitability is split equally amongst everybody because we want everybody to contribute. The bottom line is that if you can help us to be more profitable and to add more production, regardless what department it goes to, you will help the overall picture and your bonus is going to grow at the end of the year. Last year, we had one young lady that collected over $6,000 in bonuses.

Russ: On your 25% growth, how many years have you had this program in place?

Gordon: This is the third or fourth year, I believe.

Russ: How many times have you hit the 25%?

> "I just wanted to say 'Thank you' to IPS and to Quantum Club. You taught us things to promote our agency…and we are pushed to work harder and harder every single day"

Gordon: We have not hit it yet, but we did come close last year! If you sit down and run the whole numbers out and everything works the way it should, approximately $300,000 will drop to the bottom line. If we are able to do that, I am willing to give away $60,000 of that all day, every day. The bottom line is that we do share with our staff.

Russ: So do the numbers and work from there?

Gordon: Yes. That is a profitability and growth program that everyone is well aware of. This year we posted the results quarterly and got such a cry from the staff that, so we started posting it monthly. They will now know on a monthly basis and can sit down and run the numbers.

Leigh Ann: It helps departments within the agency to push other departments. For me, I am now calling producers to ask about daily calls and closing ratios. It really puts you in the game more. You want to help out everybody in the agency because if they are growing, I am growing.

Gordon: I had a salesman walk in the door the other day, and the first CSR he met said "You better be coming in here with an application."

IPS: Gordon and Leigh Ann, is there anything else before we sign off?

Leigh Ann: I just want to say 'thank you' to IPS and to Quantum Club™. You taught us things to promote our agency…and we are pushed to work harder and harder every single day.

Gordon: We belong to great groups in Quantum Club™, and it is fun to compete with those people. You better be at your best because, if you are not, they are going to be whizzing by you!

IPS: Gordon and Leigh Ann, it was a pleasure spending time with you. You are both an inspiration to everybody.

"My involvement in Quantum Club not only has given me the highest quality, hands-on, real-life tools to use in my insurance agency, but it has given me the excitement, motivation and accountability to put these tools to proper use. Michael, you taught me the IPS way of doing things. My clients have 'converted' me. They love the no-nonsense insurance information we give them in the 'High Impact Marketing' way. Thank you, Michael."
~David Collins, Springfield, MA

"Before the Quantum Club I worked 60 hours a week in the agency and had no idea why. Now I devote 8 – 10 hours a week to agency business and nearly doubled my personal income this year. Let's face it – there's only one place to go if you're a P&C agent who wants everything you can get from your business… Insurance Profit Systems."
~Joe Hagan, Jr., Birdsboro, PA

"Your training is unmatched in the insurance industry. The ability to 'pull back the curtains' and see the inner workings of the most successful agencies in the country is worth the small investment. <u>IPS has revolutionized how I approach my agency</u>. All of the tools are not in place but we are moving toward a quantum leap in how we do business."
~Jerry Kennedy, Colorado Springs, CO

"I was thinking of telling other agents in California about this, but don't want them to know! Instead I plan to buy them."
~Joseph Wilson, Long Beach, CA

Jim Janasko: Personal lines in Ohio

Jim Janasko, a long time Quantum Club™ member, now owns the agency started by his father over 50 years ago in Lorain, Ohio. After joining Quantum Club™ and instituting more efficient systems, as well as learning to delegate to the rest of his team, Jim now has the opportunity to focus on marketing and growing the business, instead of on the mundane day-to-day details. Along the way he has learned the importance of letting clients go who are not right for his agency, nurturing and retaining the clients he values and giving back to his community through charitable contributions—which he has been able to incorporate into his thriving referral program.

IPS: Hello Everyone! Thanks for joining us today. We have a great Quantum Club™ member on the line with us. He is going to be sharing some strategies on some things he did that I think are very important. He added $50,000 to the contingency. He has an unusual referral system which he has been working on very effectively and, overall, he has seen his agency go through a fairly significant transformation which has freed him up to work on his business. It has gotten him out of the drudgery of day-to-day operations and allowed him to work on things that really matter in the agency. So, it is a great story and he is a great guy. Jim Janasko, how are you?

Jim Janasko: Hello! Good afternoon. I am fine, thanks.

IPS: Alright. Let us start from the very beginning here. I would like to ask you for a little bit of a brief bio on your agency and how you got into the business.

Jim: A brief bio…I am second generation in the agency. My father started it, and it is 55 years ago this year. I came right after college and started in personal lines. My father passed away 20 years ago this month, and I have been running it on my own since then.

IPS: And where are you?

Jim: We are in Lorain, Ohio, which is thirty miles west of Cleveland. My office is about four blocks from Lake Erie.

IPS: Okay, and the overall, the makeup of the agency, is what?

Jim: The makeup is about 70% personal lines. We have our lead carrier, which is the Cincinnati Insurance

Company. If you are from the mid-west then you know that, up until about four years ago, it was totally agency billed…so we actually issued our own policies here. There was quite a bit of work with that.

IPS: *And the kind of commercial lines you have - I know you have a couple of niches, so we will dig into that in a few minutes. So, Jim, how long have you been a member of Quantum Club?*

Jim: Probably eight years.

IPS: *Okay, and in the before days? Paint a little bit of a picture because I want people to get a sense of how much your agency has changed and how your own life-style has changed. What was it like in the old days?*

Jim: In the before Quantum Club™ days it was more of an agent-driven agency or owner-driven agency, where the staff primarily answered phones, took orders, typed policies, did billing, and that was it; totally clerical. As the agency owner, I was responsible for meeting with every single customer that came through the doors. I did all of the account reviews with personal phone calls. I spent 99% of my time just talking to customers and doing service reviews.

IPS: *Okay, and how many hours a week was that?*

Jim: At that time, it was quite a bit. I was probably working 50 hours a week. Doing that sort of thing, I was newly married and not spending a lot of time at home.

IPS: *Alright, and the after story? What is it like now?*

Jim: The after story is that I have a dynamic staff that looks for new challenges on a weekly basis. They do the selling; they do the nurturing. The customers are instantly happier with them than they were with me.

IPS: *How about that. Okay. Did you get any push back on that? Were there some clients who said, you know, "That is not the way we do business…we want Jim?"*

Jim: Well, you know, that is hard, because of being a second generation and I have people that were insured as the first generation of families, so of course there are older customers that said, "Well that is not the way your father would have done this." I could retire on that one. You know, there are still some older customers that I grew up with. I mean, my dad dragged me to their kitchens, and I sat at the table, so of course I still take care of them. But we still do the old speech, "It is great talking with you, but when you have a car, Rita is the one to talk to…she takes care of it better than I do," so we had to do the speech with the customers and re-educate them.

> "In the before Quantum Club days…I was responsible for meeting with every single customer… The after story is that I have a dynamic staff… they do the selling, they do the nurturing."

IPS: *Now your customer base generally accepts that?*

Jim: Oh, absolutely!

IPS: And it is probably reflected in your retention as well.

Jim: I'm 100% sure of that.

IPS: So, the after story now. What do you do now and how is the agency different?

Jim: Now I am able to spend more of my time on marketing, and more of my time on growing the business and working on the business, not in it. If I do want to work in the business, I can pick and choose the projects that I want to. I can work in niches that I am more comfortable and more enthusiastic about instead of doing a lot of the service work. It keeps me from getting into the mundane so I can give customers the 100% that they are looking for.

IPS: What does the team consider your job to be?

Jim: Oh, they consider my job finding new niches and finding new ways to make the phone ring. That is what I am supposed to do.

IPS: And what do they think their job is?

Jim: Their job is to keep the customers happy and then to handle each and every phone call that comes to the office.

IPS: Because I know a thing or two about Rita, I am assuming that she also believes that it is her job to turn every call into a money call?

Jim: Absolutely. She was on vacation for two weeks through the holidays and, about the fourth day into her vacation, we looked at each other and said, "The phones aren't ringing. What's wrong here?" So yes, absolutely, they know that they're supposed to take care of the customers and they do an outstanding job with it.

IPS: *I want to dig into some of the specific strategies that you employed to transform your agency. You doubled your referrals, you freed up your time, and you obviously bumped your contingency up. This does go back, I think, a few years. You went through a major re-underwriting process in your agency?*

> "…in one year's time, we went from zero contingency, to a $50,000 contingency."

Jim: Yes. We had a frequency problem when I was first with Cincinnati. I was called on the carpet for that, and it was after being in Quantum Club™ for maybe a year. Now there are a lot of us members that, when we joined, we were so overwhelmed with everything that we sat back and watched and did not implement right away. Well, all of a sudden, my feet were being held to the fire. We had to do something. We started a dramatic re-underwriting of our personal lines book and that was the first "Ah Ha" moment with Quantum Club™ - finding out that you can fire a customer. That was huge and the second part, that was huge, was empowering my staff to do the firing.

IPS: *Right, and what was their reaction to that?*

Jim: At first, they were very, very, skeptical. 'That's not my job! That is why your name is on the building. You get to do those things.' Well, because I do not deal with the service, there are customers that are high maintenance that are irritating them that I know nothing about…

IPS: *And cutting into your profits.*

Jim: And yes, cutting into our profits because of loss of time and ineffective use of time.

IPS: *Not to mention the frequency problem. So you threw the monkey back on their shoulders. Okay. Maybe there was a little bit of push back but, when they accepted it, what was the reaction?*

> "…we started a dramatic re-underwriting of our personal lines book and that was the first 'Ah Ha' moment with Quantum Club - finding out that you can fire a customer."

Jim: It was fantastic; it was dynamic. The change was the first time somebody brought a file to me and said, "Look at this. This customer is all wrong for our agency because of this, and this, and this, and this. What should I do?" I said, "Can them!"

IPS: *Right. Did you advise them to direct them to another agency?*

Jim: You know we did not. We just said 'We have nothing left to offer you, so you need to go.' It really has worked out very well. We are an older steel town, so there are properties we should not be on that we got rid of. There are frequency problems; there is a hands-on service problem. Everything that takes time away from my business…I had to look at my item line-per-customer. It just was not there.

IPS: *Well, there is always some percentage of customers who are being subsidized by the other customers, so you can get rid of those and you can increase your profitability. Now, my notes, Jim, indicate that you have had four years of bad losses.*

Jim: We had a four-year frequency problem going. Finally, I had a very forceful first line supervisor, who said, 'Look at this. I've targeted this. This is what it is, so do something.' We have turned it around and, in one year's time, went from a zero contingency, to a $50,000 contingency.

IPS: *Now, did you discover anything interesting about your book of business when you went through that re-underwriting process?*

Jim: We did have a lot of mono lines due to the age of the book. Being different generation, we found that we were heavy in older neighborhoods and light in the newer neighborhoods. Even though we knew the next generation of these families, we had not gone after them as hard as we should have, so we were able to extend ourselves into the newer areas and try to 'youthfulize' our book of business.

IPS: *And you have a lot of low deductibles?*

Jim: That was the other big thing. We had people that were still carrying 25/50 limits on cars. We had $50 comp deductibles, $100 collision deductibles, and $100 homeowners. When we did the re-underwriting, we automatically bumped deductibles. We took the savings, we added things like water back-up coverage, and we rounded out the coverage more than anything. We impressed upon our customers that we are here to offer protection. Again, the key is the re-education of your customers that we're not selling a commodity.

IPS: *So, you took what was potentially a negative situation, and you got a lot of transformation and some important "Ah-Ha's" out of that?*

Jim: Absolutely.

IPS: *Okay, so you learned a lot about your book of business. You used that knowledge to actually make it better.*

Jim: Yes, definitely.

IPS: *You fired some customers and you transformed some of them; however, you want to define this as your 'A's' and 'Double A's' and the 'Triple A's.' You made better customers out of them, but you also used this as an opportunity to empower your team.*

Jim: Absolutely.

IPS: *Was Rita with you back in those days?*

Jim: Yes. Rita has been here for ten years, eleven years this month, so she was here, and she was brand new at the time and actually new to insurance, so she started the fire.

IPS: *Okay, and now I know that you place very high value on your team and you really try to nurture them just the same way we try to nurture our own client base.*

Jim: Sure. You know, we work with each other and I have told them and reminded them that we spend more time with each other than we do with our own families, so we have to work together as a team, as a family, and we have to get along. Everybody has strengths and we have to realize what each other's strengths are so we can capitalize on those.

REFERRALS

IPS: *A few years ago, Jim, you established a new referral process that generated a steady stream of referrals to the agency. Let's talk about that.*

Jim: We started with the Quantum Club™ idea of establishing a referral program, and that was something new to our customers. Again, we had to educate them because we never asked for referrals before. So we started the typical referral program with the rewards. That started off fairly slowly. What dramatically changed it in our area here was adding the charitable giving part to that.

CHARITABLE GIVING

IPS: *Tell us what you are doing there.*

Jim: We picked three local charities: the Salvation Army, a homeless shelter run by a deacon I know, and Catholic Charities, the local office. For every referral that is given to the office, there is a $5 donation split between the three. The insurance carrier came forward and gave us an extra thousand dollars and said, "You know, you've done a great job here, why don't you split this

> "We started with the Quantum Club idea of establishing a referral program, and that was something new to our customers."

between your charities, too?" That was fantastic! That was great to have a company jump on-board. Our new flyer has a picture of me with a giant check. I found online where to get the giant checks and went out and did that and got testimonials from all our charities. That doubled our referrals. We have people come in the office and, they see the posters on the walls that we have all over the front waiting area, with the big thermometer of how much we are giving and who won our big awards last year, and they really like the charitable giving. They say, 'You know, this is great that you are giving back to a community that has supported your business for so many years.'

IPS: *That is outstanding. I have a three-part formula for generating tons of referrals, so I want to break this down a little bit. Number one is that you have to nurture your client base so that they want to give you referrals. Number two is you need a program with processes, which obviously you do. Then Number three, you need constant communication and promotion of the referral campaign. How do you promote it and communicate it throughout the year?*

Jim: We put together a two-sided flyer that goes out in every piece of business and every piece of mail. That means to prospects, to customers, to company people, and to any service organization, like body shops or glass companies. Everybody gets our flyers, and my kids have them in their book bags so that everybody knows that we are out there and what we are doing for the community. We went through over 3,000 flyers last year, and that is not doing a mailing list. That is just stuffing them.

IPS: *Stuffing them?*

Jim: Yes, free postage. There is no additional cost to send them out.

CLIENT NURTURING

IPS: *Jim, what do you do to nurture the positive emotional bond with your client base? What kind of communication do they get from you throughout the year? Other than their annual premium billing?*

Jim: Other than the premium billing, we have put together three different review programs for the customers. We started out with the big two-page questionnaire. The big Quantum Club™ headline was "37% of all claims are unpaid because of insufficient coverage." We did the two-pager until it went through the whole block. Then we went to a one-pager saying, "Hey! Did we forget anything?" This year we put together a 5x8 postcard that says, "Call us, we need to review." I got it from the Quantum Club™ library. What we found is that now we can put customers on a three-year cycle so that they can get this over the three-year period that is changing. They know that we are paying attention. They know that we really care about them, and the people do mention it. They notice it: "Hey! I've never been treated this way before."

> "This year we put together a 5x8 postcard that says, 'Call us, we need to review.' I got it from the Quantum Club library."

IPS: *Now you also have another stream of referrals coming not so much from clients, but from a group of agents.*

Jim: That is an interesting one. Back to the family business—I have a guy I graduated from high school with who is a second generation State Farm agent. He calls me one day and says his best friend has teenage drivers and he cannot insure them, so will I do it for him? I said absolutely.

IPS: *And when was this?*

B2B REFERRALS

Jim: This has to be almost three years ago. Kids are in college, and turns out it is a $5,000 auto premium. I'll take it. I said, "Marty, you think you got some other agent buddies that might like the service I am providing to you? He says, "Absolutely," and we put together a list of fourteen agents; I had letters in the libraries that we solicited them with. We sent them a letter that basically said, "Hey, we are here to provide the same sort of service. We will provide for your customers the way State Farm wants it for the things you can't write, and we promise to never ever cross-sell them," which we don't. They send us a lot of commercial business.

IPS: *How do you track those clients?*

Jim: We ask every single incoming call, "How did you hear about us?" The State Farm thing has gotten so crazy that one of the CSR's from State Farm agency sends us her quote sheet. She faxes us the sheets and tells the clients, "You call Janasko and ask for Rita. She has your information, and she will have your quote ready for you," and they are calling and just blown away with it.

IPS: *You flag them in your agency management system somehow, but you never cross-sell them?*

WELCOME KIT

Jim: No. We have them all flagged that we take what we get, and it has been fantastic. We received 100 pieces of business from State Farm agents this year. I had a State Farm agent that is 30 miles away call me and ask, "Is this true what you are doing?" I said, "Yes," and he said, "I want in on it." I have never even met this guy! I sent him our Welcome Packet and he immediately sent me a piece of business.

IPS: *You have a welcome packet for State Farm agents that participate in this program?*

Jim: Right.

IPS: *What kinds of things are included in the Welcome Packet?*

Jim: We do the phone calls, or the e-mails, the e-mail addresses, our phone numbers, which companies we represent, plus a few lumpy things like a pennant and a calendar for the year, that sort of thing. The biggest thing is I do bi-monthly visits to all of the agencies.

IPS: *How many agencies?*

Jim: Fourteen agencies. And I visit them every other month because there is usually a holiday. The big thing is to find out if you send something through the mail, whether it goes to the agency principal and the staff never sees it. Now I have walked in and we put together a flyer that says, "Hey, this is what we can do for you. We write high performance boats, we do high performance motorcycles, we can do your vacant houses, with the foreclosure thing, because vacant houses are huge." I walk in with a flyer and a little box of chocolates and hand it to each-and-every staff person. We found out that those are the people that refer us. That has been fantastic. What really doubled the referrals from the State Farm agents were the visits. I did it yesterday. I saw fourteen agencies in one day. I delivered thirty-five boxes of chocolate. In the process of visiting these places, I picked up a new restaurant, a mold remediation contractor and a homeowners with frequency problems. I picked up three new pieces of business. Not just quoted, but actually sold. I mean, it was amazing, and the best part is that I walk into one and I have a logo shirt on and the lady goes, "You're Mr. Janasko." This is the staff person standing there with one of their customers. "You're him; you're the guy that sends us the candy." You have to make a personal effort with them. You have to have a relationship with the agents. I mean, it is the same as you are doing with your clients. You want referrals, so they have to know who you are.

IPS: *Well yeah, and if those fourteen are worth 100 pieces of new business last year, they are worth nurturing, aren't they?*

Jim: Absolutely! For two years in a row we have paid for the State Farm referral by April. Two-years in a row. This year, quite possibly we will have it by the end of March. We have already paid for the budget for the year, so it is a no-brainer.

IPS: *I have a note from our conversation the other day that says something about Rita. Tell us about her.*

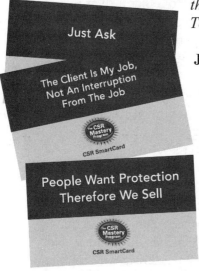

Jim: Rita is pretty amazing. She is full of personality and she is incredibly enthusiastic. The big thing in insurance has always been the fear of rejection, but she is not worried about that. It's really fun to watch her work. Since she went through the CSR Mastery Program™, she has her own little sticky things with little phrases all around her work area, so nobody gets off the phone without her either asking for an additional piece of business or a referral, one or the other. If somebody calls strictly for an auto quote, when she is done she says, "By the way, did you know you could save more if we wrote your house with it? Can I do that for you?" or if she does both of them she says, "I'm glad you are so happy with us. Do you know anybody else that would like this personal service?"

IPS: *Right on. Alright. Well kudos to you for not just recruiting her but for maintaining her and giving her an environment where she can operate at a high level of productivity. People might not know, but she was the grand-prize winner in our first "Best Year Ever Contest" for the CSR Mastery Program™.*

Jim: Number one! The first winner of the first ever CSR Mastery Program™ Contest.

IPS: Yes! She did a great job, and hopefully her numbers are still up like they were when she made her submission.

Jim: Of course they are.

IPS: Let's see Jim. You have a couple of niches and you market them with some frequency. Tell us a little something about how that works.

NICHES

Jim: We have two niches that we found a year or two ago. You gave some classes on how to find the niche. We did the meeting in Chicago with some others and basically it is two things. One that you have to have three accounts of the same business or two, that you have a personal interest in it. I came back and looked and found that we have metal fabrication shops, they are machine shops. Then we found that we have daycare centers, which they are two very odd niches to be together in the same shop. But anyway, my college degree is in organic chemistry, and in a machine shop there are plenty of chemicals. There are these big fancy machines, and I speak geek so the engineers that own the place like talking to me. Then they found out that, coincidently, we had two or three insurance companies that had programs for those niches. Well, now we are experts. Not only do we have a couple of accounts that we go to for testimonials, but we already have multiple markets in-house. I mean, we are now experts in machine shops and daycare centers, and that is how we put it together. I think in the library, my machine shop postcard is there and my daycare postcard is there.

IPS: *I seem to recall seeing them, so yes, they probably will be in the library. You mailed them, so they are a postcard campaign? Right?*

Jim: We did the postcard campaign for the last two years with pushing that program. We also do a mailing to them for workers comp and now, this year, we are doing EPLI. So now I have three pieces of their business that I can rotate through the year, so they are not seeing just the same thing. We will change the colors and we will change the format, but those are the three things that we are pushing.

IPS: *And how often do you mail to them?*

Jim: We started out once a quarter, because you know you have to put it in the budget. Once it started paying for itself, we have three pieces now for mailing; three pieces three times a year, I think, and we are doing multiple mailings of the pieces and a bunch every third month.

> "With the economy how it is, of course, your best source of new business is your existing book, and we have been working actively on cross selling."

IPS: *Where did you get your mailing list?*

Jim: We use Info USA. I do not know the pricing. It wasn't a big deal, and it is fast. You download it, and you slam it into your measurement system and go.

IPS: Okay, Jim, and what do you think you are going to do? What is on your action plan to make this coming year your Best Year Ever?

CROSS SELL

Jim: Well, we have gone back to the basics. With the economy how it is, of course, your best source of new business is your existing book, and we have been working actively on cross-selling. As a matter-of-fact, this is the fourth day that we have worked on reading through our book of business for those who do not have umbrellas. We are doing a huge umbrella campaign and we are pulling out all of our mono line homeowners; in fact, we were just going over the Joe Hagen three-letter format. That is also in the library, and it is an oldie but a goodie. In fact, we were critiquing the claims postcard just before this call happened. We were deciding if the fear factor will work in our area. You know there is stuff in the Quantum Club™ that works in some areas and does not work in others. You have to make it local.

IPS: You are looking at an umbrella campaign, and you are doing a cross-sell home-to-auto, auto-to-home?

Jim: Yes, and now that spring is coming up, we will do a toy campaign. We will look for RVs, trailers, high performance boats, and jet skis. They are big in our area, so we will make sure that everybody has all of their toys taken care of.

IPS: Okay. Anything else for the coming year that is big on your list?

Jim: Yes…annuities. If the stock market tanks, who would like to have their money guaranteed? If it goes down, I guarantee I will give you back what you gave me, so we are pushing the annuities.

IPS: *So how are you doing that?*

Jim: There is a post card, and I thought I put it in the library, I'm not sure.

IPS: *So you are mailing that to your customer base, and are you segmenting it?*

Jim: Yes, we segmented it for the first mailing, and we pulled auto policies with drivers fifty and over. Just as a test. I think we came up with 200 or 300 of those. That just went out a week or two ago, and we used the headline, "Is your nest egg coming up scrambled?" Pretty good, huh? So we found out there is another promotion the United Postal Service has, *"click to mail."* You take your postcard, and they have a template so you make sure that it fits. You upload your artwork, you upload your mailing list in Excel format, pick the day you want it to go out, and it is all done. It is so incredibly easy. That was back to the old Tom Larsen, and you can find it at clicktomail.com. They send me e-mails to say it is in production, they send me e-mails to say it has been mailed, and they send it to me so I can see it. They scrub the list and they tell you, "Hey…these guys do not have addresses that fit our format. What do you want to do with them?" It really is as easy as it gets, and they save everything so you can just click 'send' to send it again.

IPS: *And upload a new list?*

Jim: You can upload a new list, or you can keep your old list, and you can send them a new piece to just upload your new artwork. That is definitely the easiest way to go.

IPS: *That is a great service. Okay Jim, in a moment I will open it up for questions and our operator Kerry will tell everyone how they can do that. Is there anything else you want to add?*

Jim: No, I think that is it. We have the stuff we are doing now, and I bragged about my terrific, outstanding staff that gives me the freedom to do what I want to do, when I want to do it. That is the one thing - if you do not have people around you that you like working with, forget it. Also, I will answer e-mail questions if I said anything that was worthwhile.

IPS: Kerry, do we have any questions or comments for Jim?

Kerry: We do have our first question, and it comes from Tamara from Washington. Tamra, your line is opened.

IPS: Hi, where you calling from?

Tamara: Danwood, Washington. I would like to know if you compensate all of the State Farm agents that give you referrals.

Jim: No, I do not work with commission, but we do the exact same thing we do for our normal referral program. We send down lottery tickets for the referral, and we have a quarterly drawing for a gas card and we have an annual drawing for a $250.00 Visa gift card.

Tamara: Okay, great.

Jim: You can bet that the staff from each of the offices knows who won it last year. They are into it.

IPS: So the promotion and communication is really important?

Jim: Absolutely!
Kerry: Our next question comes from Geri in Arizona. Geri, your line is open.

Geri: I was not going to let this call go by without asking a couple of questions. You mark this in your management system, when you say that you freeze referrals that are State Farm agent referrals? How do you do that?

Jim: I have to keep an eye out for that—I know there is a little box that says marketing programs. It goes there as a State Farm referral. Then, up in the note section, we will actually put which State Farm agent sent that. It says 'State Farm,' and I think they put it in parentheses, 'see note,' so then you look up there and see who sent it.

Geri: Okay, That is a really good idea. Then you can run a report to show which State Farm agents and which account it was applied to and so forth, right?

Jim: Exactly.

IPS: Okay, that is all the time we have—thank you Jim for sharing.

Joel Zwicker: Personal lines in Nova Scotia, Canada

Joel Zwicker, a Quantum Club™ member since 2006, started off in the golf industry but eventually realized it wouldn't provide a sufficient livelihood for him. He saw the insurance industry as a better alternative, and now works for AA Monroe Insurance, a $30 million agency, at an office in the Annapolis Valley in Nova Scotia, Canada. Before joining Quantum Club™, Joel felt very discouraged and uncertain about his future in the industry. As a young man, he knew he would have about 30 more years doing this job, and the way things were going at his agency, selling a mere 114 policies in 7 months, he didn't see how there would be a future for him there. After joining Quantum Club™ however, Joel viewed the future with much more optimism; using the new techniques he learned, his agency now sells that many policies in a matter of 3 or 4 weeks instead of months.

IPS: *So Joel, you have become something of shining star at your agency. How do they look at your production? Your fast growing branch? Your nontraditional advertising & marketing?*

Joel Zwicker: When I first started, the owner and I started trying out some new strategies and tracking the numbers. I was asked to go and do a presentation to the Principals of the company. I showed them what we'd been doing, and I got crapped on, for lack of a better word. With the exception of the owner and maybe one other guy, everybody said "you can't say this; you can't do this" and I was like "why not?" You've been doing it this way for 60 years and you're losing business, so why not try some other way. You know what? This is my life; it's my 30 years I have to put into this, so let's try it my way; if you don't like it, you can fire me in a year. Well, we're still here.

IPS*: That reminds me…you posted something interesting on Qmail earlier today. It was a list of things that a Producer that does between $750,000 and a million dollars a year in new business. He won't: 1. Call a referral. 2. Cold call. 3. Leave his office for anything other than golf and fishing. 4. Send a marketing piece that doesn't get at least 4 to 1 ROI (Return on Investment). 5. Let anyone, and I mean anyone, tell him "you can't do that or you can't say that." And you are that guy. You're doing close to a million dollars in new business and these are not huge policy premiums out there, are they?*

Joel: Here in the Annapolis Valley where I am, I can give somebody with a $250,000 or $350,000 rebuilt house the absolute best homeowners policy, with flood and everything, million dollars liability, you name it; the cat's meow policy with a $500 deductible for about $500.

IPS: And that would maybe be a million dollar home or more in California?

Joel: Exactly.

IPS: Okay, so let's back up to the beginning; how long have you been active in Quantum Club™?

Joel: Since February of 2006.

IPS: How long were you active as an agent before that?

Joel: 7 months.

IPS: So what were those 7 months like?

Joel: Scary. We did nothing, to be honest with you. In 7 months, we did 114 policies.

IPS: Okay. So how were the next 30 years looking to you then?

Joel: Bleak. Truthfully I really believe that at that time if they really wanted me with that company, they would ask me to transfer or I may be looking for job again. Scary when you have a kid and another one on the way.

IPS: Okay. So 114 policies in your first 7months pre-Quantum Club™, and now how long does it take you to add another 114 policies?

Joel: 3 weeks, 4 weeks.

IPS: So now how do the next 30 years look to you?

Joel: Look real good. I think that's enough said.

IPS: *Obviously, Joel is a young guy looking to a career here. I would say he's got a long, very bright future ahead of him. So let's take a look at some of the things that you implemented that have had a big payoff for you.*

TRACKING NUMBERS

Joel: What got the ball rolling here was tracking the numbers. That was so key, because we knew what we were doing and knew it wasn't working, but then when we started to implement new strategies, we could see which ones were actually working and continue to use those. If you're sending out 10 or 15 things and you're not tracking, you may just say to yourself, WOW! Look at how well that's working! But if you tracked the numbers, you might find out that only 3 of those 15 things are actually working. So then you can really chop the, I hate the word budget, but you can chop the expenditures on marketing when you know those 3 things work; you know then you don't need the other 12; then you find the next few things

> "What got the ball rolling here was tracking the numbers. That was so key, because we knew what we were doing and knew it wasn't working, but then when we started to implement new strategies, we could see which ones were actually working and continue to use those."

that work. So the first thing we found that really worked well for us was a flyer campaign. I think the number one most important thing that any new Quantum Club™ member can know about is the flyers: it took us 7 attempts to get one that worked. It wasn't as simple as going into the library and finding somebody else's flyer that worked well for them and sending it out in our area. Those flyers worked somewhere else, but you have to adapt it to your market, your region. So you have to implement it, tweak it, track it.

IPS: What were some of the changes that you made that made it more successful in your market place?

Joel: We used headlines, and when I say "headlines," I mean one or two words, not sentences. And the sub-headline we are using now is "simply the best". The same goes for titling testimonials; for example, if you're doing a flyer about saving money, include a testimonial titled "saved $2600". Those are the small changes that make the difference between getting a lot of calls and getting an insane amount of calls.

> "I think the number one most important thing that any new Quantum Club member can know about is the flyers...."

IPS: And are you still mailing the same flyer? Do you have a control piece that's been steady for you?

MARKET TESTING

Joel: The flyer goes every month. We send 20,000 every month and we've had two flyers. We just had one that went for a year and a half and it started to taper off; we were getting like 7 to 1 return on that one. When we first started with it, it was constantly 7 to 1, but then it dropped down to 4 to 1 return and so we thought, "let's change it up," do something new. So we changed it up and now we are back up to 7 to 1.

IPS: Right on, and was it the change in the headline or change in the testimonials? Which was it?

Joel: We started to look at the headline, which we changed, and we changed the subhead. We started to use the power of AA Monroe Insurance as a whole as opposed to using the power of only our individual office. We tried to make ourselves feel big by putting big numbers out there; like saying for example, we have 21,000 clients. Given that there are only about 20,000 people in the county, which sounds pretty impressive. So people realize, "well gee…these guys are for real."

IPS: So how big is your territory? Because you have like 15 other branches that to some extent, you're competing with.

Joel: Well, we actually have 17 offices now in the province and the province of Nova Scotia only has a population of 900,000. The closest office to me, now…I'm a little bit lucky, is about an hour and 15 minutes away on the other side of Halifax. And my territory here in the valley consists of around 75,000 people. And that's in a stretch of about an hour and a half of highway driving.

IPS: So, how do you get the list for that 20,000?

Joel: We are lucky; we have a business called "Flyer Services" that we use. Basically, every Saturday, they deliver flyers directly to homes in packets, and that's how we distribute our flyers. We used the postal service before and it wasn't working for us, so we tried this flyer service and it took our numbers up to where we wanted them, because the flyer was getting to the right houses, bundled with 30, 40 or 50 other flyers.

> "...the first change I would make at any agency is make sure you have a referral program...we did half a million dollars off of referrals. That's astronomical. I couldn't believe it."

IPS: They are bundled, so you get cheap delivery, but you also get the competing flyer factor.

Joel: True, we have the competing flyer factor, but the people that get them are the people who want them because Flyer Services only delivers to people who want the flyers.

IPS: So every Saturday, how many flyers go out? 5,000 a week? Or do you do 20,000 all at once?

Joel: No, we don't do them all at once because we don't want to run ourselves ragged...we used to do that, and we would get 400 incoming calls, and we couldn't answer so many. So we send out different numbers depending on the communities; we average around 7,000 a week. But some of the areas are smaller so we might only send 4,000; it just depends on the size of the community.

REFERRALS

IPS*: What other tools have you used? As for your referral campaign, in the beginning you didn't really have the opportunity for a lot of referrals; you didn't have a lot of clients.*

Joel: No, we were foolish then. But now, the best part about the referral program is that new clients refer more than anybody. Right? And that's because those people are happy, they are excited about you; they just came in, and you just doubled their coverage or saved them money, so they like you. So they are most likely to refer. So the first change I would make at any agency is making sure you have a referral program. Even if there's nobody coming in the door at that moment, because you want to have that established the minute the people really start coming in. I just checked the numbers from last year, we did half a million dollars off of referrals. That's astronomical. I couldn't believe it. We give away two 42" TV's a year as a reward for referrals. We would grow this business by 50% every year by not doing any marketing other than the referral program.

IPS*: Right on, and your referral program sounds like it's more or less the standard QC contest style, with a shiny new TV as the reward?*

Joel: Shiny new TV and we send a thank you card to every referral. We used to give stuff away, but then I had to start paying for it, and I didn't think it was worth it. I thought the TV should be enough and it was. But we are only one office of 16, so when everybody saw us doing big referrals, they said "oh geez!" I'll go buy a TV. It's not that simple; everybody in your office, or in your agency, has to be on-board. Every phone call has to end with, "don't forget to refer; we'll try to get you a TV."

IPS: *What are the means that you use to communicate with your marketplace? And I assume that there's a message about referrals in a lot of these, but also what are the methods through which you nurture your existing client base?*

Joel: We have the newsletter, obviously. The last page of that is always dedicated to referrals. We have enough policies that we don't talk anything insurance in the newsletter. I believe that we are in the relationship business and in order to create a relationship with someone, you need to be able to relate to each other in some way. So in our newsletter, we show our staff doing client-like things. We want to show our clients that we are just the average guy…for example, in June the son of one of our staff won MVP in a hockey tournament, and we included that in the newsletter. Why? Because we have kids, too. We are just the average guy in the average town doing what you do. Showing that in the newsletter helps build those relationships with clients because then they feel they can relate to us.

IPS: *And are you e-mailing your clients?*

Joel: We do a broad e-mail at least once a month. We don't do as much because we don't have a huge database of e-mails. That's one thing that we were not good at when we first started, we just started to pick up on those in the last year. Basically, any new client over the last year, we have their email but anyone before that; we are busting our chops getting those.

IPS: Are you a ZipDrip™ account user?

Joel: Yes.

IPS: Okay, I wanted to take a look at the way you're promoting your TV contest. You mention it in the monthly newsletter, and then of course you reward the people every time they make a referral by sending a thank you...

> "...and every phone call ends with 'don't forget to send your friends for our referral contest."

Joel: Every desk in the office has "win a free TV...ask for details," and every phone call ends with "don't forget to send your friends for our referral contest."

IPS: Do you get much walk in business? Is there a lot of face to face?

Joel: Oh yes! We are in a small area. A lot people want to deal with you face to face, and of course when you drive up to the office, the first thing you see is we have two huge windows, and one of them is entirely dedicated to referral rewards. There are pictures of the most recent winners with the TV, almost life size on the window. Anyone who drives by sees this, and when you drive in you see it. Then, of course, the TV is there. Every piece of outgoing mail has a stuffer in it about the referral rewards. We have all our companies that we deal with that send the policies directly to the client put stickers and the stuffers in there for us. So it's not just agency bill customers that are getting the stuffers, it's the direct bill, too. Every e-mail. You name it.

IPS: *Unless you have already done this, if you can take a digital picture of your front window and post it on Qmail, I know that people would love to see that.*

Joel: Absolutely, absolutely

IPS: *Other than the referral program, as I recall, your closing ratio on referrals is very, very high.*

Joel: 89% on referral business.

IPS*: Not bad.*

Joel: 89%, yeah, that's great! I didn't know it was that high, to be honest with you.

IPS: *No, not bad at all, so that's the whole campaign that would qualify it as a homerun. ROI on that is a grand slam.*

Joel: Part of the program.

IPS*: Okay, so now in addition to that, you've got your flyers. And you are also using some sort of interesting ways of positioning your agency…you could call it branding. You developed a personality around the agency itself. Can you tell us a little bit about that?*

BRANDING

Joel: Well, we opened an office that was one of 16 in a place where there were a lot of other offices around that had been here for a long time. They were staples of the community, if you will. So you have an office, you have your agency called AA Monroe Insurance, the Insurance Specialist. My question was who cares? Who cares who AA Monroe is? I care and the people who work here care, but the reality is that people in the community don't really care. Right? They need something that they can latch onto, especially because we are a brokerage that came from another community. So when we started to build the business, and people were coming in, they would always say to us, "Hey, do you guys have a sharp pencil or can you sharpen it up there for me?" It's not just in this business, you can go to a contractor and say "hey, sharpen your pencil for me, buddy." So, you know what? We coined it. We coined it and we coined "home of the sharpest pencil in town". And everything we do now has to do with the sharpest pencil in town, to the point that when you walk downtown or any one of the towns around and you say "Who's got the sharpest pencil in town?" people will tell you, AA Monroe Insurance. You don't even have to be talking about insurance and people will say AA Monroe Insurance.

IPS: Alright, so what are the ways that they get that message? Because clearly you've made that stick in their heads.

NEWSLETTERS

Joel: Well, thanks to Quantum Club™ members, we have a mascot, who we call "Hector the Protector". We had a naming contest with clients. Clients emailed, mailed or brought in their ideas to name the pencil guy, and the winner was "Hector the Protector". We have a life size cut out in the office and he sits out by the side of the road.

This past spring, we had a parade entry into the Apple Blossom Parade, which is the largest and oldest grand street parade in Canada. We actually had a client help carve a 24-foot pencil that needed to be hauled around the parade by a crane. And, of course, we threw over 15,000 pencils with AA Monroe insurance "home of the sharpest pencil in town" into the crowd. We threw hundred's of tee shirts with "the sharpest pencil in town" written on them. All these things, everything we do, pushes the idea of the sharpest pencil in town.

IPS: Quantum Club™ members can get on Qmail and see a posting that Joel made with a picture of him with the 20-foot pencil and the truck that is hauling it; it's really quite amazing.

Joel: Now we've taken that pencil, and we've sort of tidied it up a little bit, made it so it would last longer, and we're waiting for the welding company to come and put a new platform on the outside of the new offices. We are actually going to erect that pencil to the outside of the offices.

IPS: That's outstanding.

Joel: That will make it very easy for anyone to find us.

IPS: *Okay. So that's a personality and an image for the agency that you could probably stick with for 30 years because it's visually memorable and sticks in the brain and in the marketplace.*

Joel: Yeah, it's to the point now that we've branded this office, and there are about 5 other offices with the name of AA Monroe Insurance that are sort of jumping on that band wagon.

IPS: *How are the other branch managers looking at you, because obviously none of them are growing at the pace you're growing at? What are they thinking about this guy who came from the golf industry and didn't know anything about insurance? Struggled for 7 months then all of a sudden shot through the stratosphere?*

Joel: I think they are starting to get it. First I think they're like, "who is this guy? What is he doing? We can't do this, we can't try this stuff; we've been here forever." But that doesn't mean they can't change, it just takes more than one person. Like I say, AA Monroe Insurance has referral programs in virtually every office, so you can imagine—we give away 2 TVs here, but how many TVs for 16 offices. Right? They are starting to get that the referral program is really important. Now with the first few TVs, they weren't getting any referrals, so we had these branch managers call and say, "We have TV's here and it's not happening". But like I said, it's not that easy. If it was that easy, everybody would do it. You could just give away 50 TV's. But the problem is that you have to nurture the relationships and train your clients, especially if you have a large agency that has a lot of existing clients. You have to retrain those people to refer. Those people have been there with you for 20 years and you've never asked them to do anything but to come and pay their bill and update a few files once in awhile. So you have to retrain them to now tell everybody about you, and here's why: because you're going to give them a TV.

IPS: *Got it. Now there is another technique you use that, frankly, is odd; it's unusual… we call it the real-estate sign. Do you have a picture of this loaded up into the library?*

Joel: Yes, I think there is an old one, I don't know if there's a new one, but I certainly will attach some stuff to Qmail today. Basically, there is one thing that we notice with the flyers; you never know who is going to walk in the door with it. It could be high end, low end, high risk, low risk. You don't know. So we did a search through our books and we notice we were getting some great clients, but we really weren't getting anything from the high-end neighborhoods. There's like a half a dozen high-end neighborhoods around here that we had a few clients in, but we weren't getting the numbers like in other communities. So we decided maybe there was something we could do to go after them, we developed a different newsletter campaign. It looks like a newsletter but it's really an ad, and we used a few things from the Quantum Club™ library for it. Now we send those out once a month in the high-end neighbors and it will say, for example, one of the neighborhoods is Fox Hill, so the newsletter that goes to that neighborhood says "Fox Hill Times." It looks like a newsletter for that neighborhood. We know on the first week of every month, Fox Hill is getting the newsletter, so we make sure that we have 2 or 3 or as many as possible of our real estate signs in those neighborhoods when they are getting the newsletter in the mail. And this is direct mail, not flyers. So they are getting the newsletter, and whether they are reading it or not, the next thing you know is their neighbor is putting a real estate sign up. Basically, what the real estate sign is, mimicking the idea of a real estate agent who gets to put their sign on your lawn for free advertising for however long it takes them to sell your house. Then, when they do sell it, they get to put a sold sign on it and they leave it on there a little bit longer and you have to pay them god knows how much to do that. So my theory is I actually have done something for these people when I sell them coverage. I've provided protection for the things that they love the most and maybe even saved them a little money in doing it, so why can't I put my sign on their lawn for a week or two?

IPS: *So how many of these signs might go up in the Fox Hill neighborhood?*

Joel: In Fox Hill on the morning the newsletter is delivered, I've had up to 4 signs; typically, we have 2 or 3 but I've had up to 4.

IPS: *And how do you get the people to say "Okay, put a sign on my lawn"?*

Joel: It's a really neat thing that we do. We ask. It's amazing what people will do if you just ask.

IPS: *Are they brand new clients, so there's that high emotional buzz? Or are they like long-term clients and you're just asking?*

> "On this high-end neighborhood newsletter campaign, our ROI is 4 to 1."

Joel: A little bit of both. You don't want them on the same lawns every week, so you might have someone you sold insurance to for years put it up.

IPS: *I think it's brilliant. You're doing this in high-end homeowner communities?*

Joel: That's right. If, for some reason, if there's a week there's no newsletter going out for that week, we will go around to other neighborhoods, but predominately in those neighborhoods.

IPS: *How often do those newsletters go out?*

Joel: They go out 3 weeks of the month. We cover all 6 subdivisions in 3 weeks.

IPS: *Got it. So they will get a newsletter in their neighborhood once a month? And it's customized for their neighborhood, so at least you change the banner or the headline of the newsletter?*

Joel: Exactly. Basically, it's the same newsletter for the all subdivision; the only thing we change is the name of the newsletter.

IPS: *And is it the same newsletter that your clients get?*

Joel: No. It's stuff about homeowners insurance, auto insurance. For example, why do I need collision? You know a lot of the clients have got a lot of money; they have the nineteen eighty something BMW, why do they need collision for it? Why does their kid need renters insurance when he goes off to a university?

IPS: *How many pages is it?*

Joel: It's just a fold over of a typical letter size.

IPS: *So it's a two-sided 8 ½ by 11? But one side has mailing information on it so it's One and a half pages of content?*

Joel: One and a half pages of content and the bottom of the backside is the contact information. A copy of that is in the library.

IPS: *And there is a PDF of your sign, but it would be fun if you actually had a digital picture so people can just relate to the fact that you're actually putting these out there. I think its fun; I think it's an incredible concept.*

Joel: Yeah, I'll try to take a picture whenever we stick the sign on someone's lawn. We try to take a picture every time so we have it when we are doing referrals, we can have them rolling in the background. We have pictures of the real-estate signs, the referral give-away and the large pencils and stuff.

IPS*: So in your newsletters that go out to the high-end neighborhoods, I assume each article ends with some call to action or some way to find you?*

Joel: I think the current one is the one we call the 'dirty little secrets trick.'

IPS*: Five dirty little secrets about homeowners insurance.*

Joel: Yep, then on the back it just says "call today for your free home protection quote that won't leave you with dirty little secrets."

IPS*: Right, now because the premiums are obviously a little higher here, do you know what your ROI is on this campaign?*

Joel: On this high-end neighborhood newsletter campaign, our ROI is currently 4 to 1.

IPS: *And how many are you mailing out? How big is the market for this?*

Joel: There is only a grand total of about eighteen hundred.

IPS: *So eighteen hundred of these go out per month. Alright, is there anything else we need to cover? Your retention is good.*

Joel: Well it is now. Last year at this time it wasn't…

RETENTION

IPS: *So what are the changes you made to improve retention?*

Joel: CSR Mastery Program™, CSR Mastery Program™ and CSR Mastery Program™.

IPS: *Well thanks, I wasn't looking for a plug on that, but thanks.*

> "So what are the changes you made to improve retention?"
>
> "– CSR Mastery Program, CSR Mastery Program and CSR Mastery Program."

Joel: 13% increase this year on retention. As proud as I am when you say we grew 62% and all that, to me this increase in retention is massive. That is massive to go from 78% retention to 91%; then you know you're getting better.

IPS: *So what about looking to the future, like to the next 12 months. What is on your plan of action?*

Joel: In the next couple of months, I'm moving. The office is going to stay on autopilot, if you will; I'm opening another from-scratch office, in another town that's a little closer to my hometown. My grandfather passed away this past year and he meant the world to me, and my grandmother is still there. They've never asked me for anything in life, but they have given me everything. She needs someone there, so I'm going to go down there and I'm going to open an office so that I can be close to her. It's really exciting for me, because how many times have you said "if I only knew then what I know now." I think, is going to be really fun. I won't have to wait for seven months to start seeing results. You know, because even once you figure out, "Oh, there's a thing called Quantum Club™ or Insurance Profit Systems™," it still takes you 2 or 3 months to figure out everything from there too. So now the first year we can hit the ground running. I mean, we have every intention to do blitz marketing before we even open the office and start branding the "sharpest pencil in town" down there. Then if we open the doors of that office and in the first month, we don't do at least 100 pieces of new business, I will be disappointed.

> "13% increase this year on retention. As proud as I am when you say we grew 62% and all that, to me this increase in retention is massive. That is massive to go from 78% retention to 91%"

IPS: *And how confident are you that your existing office will run well on autopilot?*

Joel: Not a doubt in my mind.

IPS: Okay. Joel, unless you have anything else, we can see whether or not the members that are on the line have questions for you.

Joel: Absolutely, fire away.

IPS: Joel covered a lot of ground here so, let's hear what people have to say. Alright Shane, do we have anybody?

Shane: Yes, we sure do. The first one is from Gary in North Carolina. Go ahead Gary.

Gary: Good afternoon gentlemen. This is Gary.

IPS: Gary, how are you.

Gary: Great; great. Joel, good to talk to you. My grand-pappy used to have a saying "it ain't bragging if you're doing it" so Kudos' to you! You're doing a great job. I've got a question, could you elaborate more on what specifically you think has helped increase your retention?

Joel: It's the ability of the people answering the phone to cross-sell the business, in my opinion. Our cross-sales have gone up a lot and you know there is a statistic that tells it all: if a client has one policy, they will stay 30% of the time. And that's one thing that I start to notice when I look at every policy that we lose. I look at them because I want to know why we lost it. If we did something wrong, I just want to know. Typically, right now the only time we are losing someone is when they only have one policy, because we didn't cross-sell at the time that we started covering them. Knowing what to say, how to say it and how to close a deal on a cross-sale—which my CSR's learned from the CSR Mastery Program™—is very important. It has been a huge part of that increase in retention.

Gary: Great, great! Thank you.

IPS: Okay, keep up the good work and look forward to seeing you at the marketing summit.

Gary: We will be there.

> "Knowing what to say, how to say it and how to close a deal on a cross-sale—which my CSR's learned from the CSR Mastery Program—is very important. It has been a huge part of that increase in retention."

IPS: Alright, good to talk to you Gary.

Gary: Thank you

IPS: Shane, anybody else?

Shane: Next is Jenn, also in North Carolina, go ahead.

Jenn: Hi Joel; great comments, really exciting. I have a question about your flyer program. What are your selection criteria and what is your competing flyer factor?

Joel: Selection criteria; explain to me what exactly you want there.

Jenn: In other words, apparently you're using someone to do your mailing for you for your flyer, and I think you said you send out like 5,000 a month? Do you have certain criteria for who they go to, for example, "I want to be in this market, I want them to go to homes that are a hundred and fifty thousand and above?" And to people with good credit? Do you have some control over that?

Joel: I don't and, even if I did, I wouldn't because with this flyer I'm going after anybody and everybody. It's what I call "shot gun" or drag netting. Basically, if they are willing to call then I want to talk to them about that flyer. I don't have the ability to control who gets it; the only part I have the ability to control is I can pick what small community I send it to, and some towns obviously are more affluent then others, but with that I send it out to everybody.

Jenn: And what is this competing flyer factor, what is that?

IPS: That was the phrase I just coined. It's a disadvantage that Joel has in his situation because his flyer gets delivered with 20 or 30 other flyers. It's the Val-pack factor. So there are probably flyers for dry cleaning and pizza and discounts at the local restaurants and movies and that kind of jazz. Do you see what I'm saying?

Jenn: Is it in a booklet format?

Joel: My flyer is its own individual flyer. It's printed on the goldenrod, the orange with black text. When you open the packets they all fly everywhere, so what makes yours stand out? A. it's the color; B. what it says in the headline; you have to catch their attention. In my opinion, you have two or three words to catch them, and then let them read the rest. There is other stuff in there that people are looking for, but there is no other insurance agency and even if there is, their flyer isn't half of what ours is and it's not saying the right thing.

IPS: Jenn, he has a trade off. He can deliver more cheaply just like you can deliver, let's say, in a Val pack more cheaply, but he traded off on the fact that there is a lot of other stuff coming out of the envelope at the same time. And he can't target even if he wanted to but, in this case, he doesn't.

Joel: And because we can't target those flyers, we developed our high-end homeowners program to just target those neighborhoods. We found a media funnel, the neighborhood newsletters, to target those places and that's the route we go. It costs us more but, with the other flyers, it's only 10 cents printed and delivered, so we're able to do it.

Jenn: Wow! That's cheap. And do you find one better than the other? The value pack versus the higher-end route using a selection process?

IPS: No. There are so many variables in the marketplace. I mean, even Joel took
things that were working fabulously well in another community and he had to tweak it before it really hit the homerun for him. There are just too many variables on that for me to be able to flat out say "I know which one works better in which community." You follow me?

Jenn: Yes. Thank you guys.

IPS: That's why as Joel stressed, testing and measuring is so important in what we do. Okay? Shane?

Shane: Next up is Tom in Pennsylvania, go ahead.

Tom: Hey, thanks so much for this great, great information over the past hour. I just have a couple of questions; I'm brand new to QC, not even a month yet.

IPS: Well, welcome.

Tom: Thank you. I'm starting a brand new scratch agency without P & C (property
and casualty) experience. I have life now in the background. You have mentioned a couple of things to me and I'm excited.

IPS: Yeah, we were just talking about you yesterday. What city are you in?

Tom: Birdsboro.

IPS: Yes, fabulous, the Mecca of insurance marketing, Birdsboro, Pennsylvania.

Tom: That's right; I'm right down the road from Joel.

IPS: Once you're with Joel for a while, you can't go wrong.

Tom: Yeah, I have a big shadow. You know, I've talked to him about some crazy ideas that I'm doing. I thought I could do this before QC, and now I know I can do it, but

I'm like a kid in a candy store. Joel, you're starting a scratch agency near where your grandma lives, and you got an existing brand behind you, but I don't. I wanted to see what you're planning to do. I know you're going to kind of duplicate what you've done. What would you recommend to someone like me who is new to the marketplace? I feel like I can do this, but you also mentioned the bad word of marketing, budget, early on. I'm trying not to go out of control on that.

Joel: My thing is I hate the word budget because I don't think you should have one. If you have something that's working, don't stop spending. Just keep going, right? But you have to know whether it's working or not. As far as what I'm going to do, I have an existing brand, though it's not really a brand down there yet, as they don't know who we are. The key is that we are building relationships. You know you can call this the protection business and you can call it the insurance business, but the reality is that people are going to come to you and stay with you because of a relationship. If they can't find something to bond with you over, and it's not going to be insurance, they won't stay. Whether it's a name, a trademark, a picture, a mascot, or it's the sharpest pencil in town, whatever it is you have to find it and just pound it into their head. For example, coca-cola has only had two jingles, or trademarks, if you will, in how many years? Why? Because they just use the same line over and over and beat that into everybody, and that's not going to happen in a day. I was lucky that it took us a year to get to the position we are now and, let me tell you,

> "I thought I could do this before QC, and now I know I can do it...."

there was a lot of money spent in that year, but I think it was well worth it.

Tom: That's cool guys, thank you very much.

IPS: I like the way Joel put it, beat it into them. Just a word about branding—you do want to be careful about global corporation style branding where they can't possibly measure their ROI. Most of the advertising is done by an outside advertising agency that gets paid by how much advertising they purchase, not by what the ROI is on the advertising that they purchase. Small businesses will go broke if they only do branding. What Joel has done is he has successfully merged the two. I prefer to call it positioning with direct response. The lesson is you can actually create a position or create a brand and make money at the same time by integrating it with direct response or high impact marketing. Shane, do we have any more questions?

Shane: Certainly, next is Shawn in Alabama.

Shawn: Thanks for taking my call; my question is, in order for you to get this agency from scratch to selling 100 policies in a month, how much money are you're going to have to invest?

Joel: Let me make a quick calculation here and then I can tell you. Plus two TV's. Thirty thousand bucks is what I will spend in the first year.

IPS: And how much will you get back for those thirty thousand dollars?

Joel: A quarter of million.

Shawn: That's good.

IPS: And how long will you keep those clients?

Joel: Forever. That's the plan at least.

IPS: Alright, does that answer your question?

Shawn: Yes sir.

Michael: Alright, very good. Shane do we have anything else?

Shane: Yes, we have Bob in Canada, go ahead Bob.

Bob: Hey Joel how are you?

Joel: Good

Bob: I'm in Sussex, not too far from you. A question for you, I'm new as well to Quantum Club™ and I want to get started in the referral program. How long did you have to pay for your referrals? I know now that you're doing it by just paying for a card.

> "You will get more calls from that hand written thank you note than you ever will from a free motor vehicle inspection."

Joel: Well, I never actually paid; I stopped before that. What I did is that there are other businesses out there nearby, so for example, in my office here right across the street is a repair shop and I would go knock on the door and say "hey listen, we have this referral program…is there something you can do?" So he gave me a stack of complimentary motor vehicle inspections. So we gave those away until we ran out. Then I ran down the road to

Copyright © 2010

the next guy and said "hey listen; this is what this guy did; do you think you could do something else?" And you know what? He gave me coupons for 100 personal pan pizzas. So I gave those away with the referral thank you cards. But then I ran out of 'free this' or 'free that,' so I started to say "you know what? I really don't have the time nor do I want to go ask for stuff," so you know what? Let's not do it. Let's just send them a hand written note thanking them. I don't remember which Quantum Club™ member originally said it, just a hand written thank you note is enough, and people will love it. So decided to just get some thank you cards made out with the company logo on the inside with "thanks a million for your referral." Now we just write a hand written note: "Hey! Appreciate the referral. Keep up the good work! Hopefully we give you a TV some day. Thanks from Joel." You will get more calls from that hand written thank you note then you ever will from a free motor vehicle inspection!

Bob: Sounds good.

IPS: Alright, Shane, do we have anybody else?

Shane: Yes we do; we have Jerry, also from Canada. Jerry go ahead.

Jerry: Oh hi, I'm in central Canada in Winnipeg, so I'd like to say hi to my fellow Canadian. Joel, closing ratios on your referral program are astonishing: 89% and 81% on new business. We do a lot of niche products in the commercial side out here and boy, if I could get 7 or 8 out of 10 in what we are doing! We are in a bit of a wholesale town. I was just kind of curious on what are some of the things to keep that competitive edge so that your closing ratio is so fantastic?

Joel: You know our thing is that, number one; you get off the price battle field. As much as you want to be competitive in price, the last thing we want to do is get into the habit of doing that on a day to day basis and all of a sudden, find out we're not competitive. So you have to put some value into what you're selling. We discuss every policy that we haul in here and look at it and I tell everybody, "Find what's wrong." There's something wrong; there must to be something wrong with it or something we can improve. If they only have 1 million in coverage then we provide 2 million. If they don't have single limited then we give them single limited. If they have broad form then we quote comprehensive and we explain why, right? That means the number one thing is get off the price battle field and provide value to those people and also, have fun. For god sakes, people are so sick of walking in places that people are all high and mighty, saying "I work at the insurance brokerage" or "I work at the bank and I'm better than you." You know, nobody cares. Be a person. Sit there and talk about everything under the sun other than insurance and you will close the deal. The minute you start talking about insurance, you're going to lose them. Why? Because you're the insurance professional, so you know the right protection to give them. Explain to them that you're going to quote this because this is better and here's why. How's the weather today? I'm going to quote you with a thousand dollar deductible, not a five thousand dollar deductible, because it will provide you with a 12% discount. How are your kids? That's what I do.

Jerry: Yeah, well that's fantastic and I know we are trying to get out of the price race a little bit and get more into value-added, especially in the commercial side. Our niche products are so comprehensive, as I understand, that in some cases nobody touches us in there, but it always seems to come down to price: "Yeah, you're a great guy Jerry and all that, but you know I can still save five hundred thousand dollars and your prices are a little too high." Yeah, I think you're right and I think we need to get off the prices now.

IPS: If you're going to compete on price, you're going to die on it, if you don't have it. Just because they walk in with that paradigm doesn't mean that you get stuck in it. You just have to get out of the price box.

Jerry: Thank you very much for the information.

IPS: Alright then, I want to thank everybody for joining us. I love you all. I admire the fact that each and every one of you took the time out of your schedule because I know you're busy. Hopefully you got a lot of value out of this. I've got three pages of notes, so you know, I'm sure you did. Regardless of what niche you're in or whether you do personal or commercial lines, listen closely to the principles, because that's what Joel has really mastered here. He's really mastered the principle that makes this work. So to you Joel, I want to say thanks for the generosity and congratulations on your success.

Joel: It's an honor.

Shaun Irwin: Commercial lines in Minnesota

Shaun Irwin, a Quantum Club™ member since 2000 and winner of the first IPS Best Year Ever contest in 2005, now runs three businesses in addition to his insurance agency in Minnesota. Implementing The Quantum Process Designers™ and strategies have allowed him to get out of the drudgery of day-to-day operations and focus on the aspects of the business he most enjoys, like marketing. It has also allowed him to spend more time with his family and be more involved in his children's lives—he now never misses a sports game or recital. He has also seen the importance of investing in his employees to make sure they want to continue working for him, and has developed a unique employee-nurturing and retention program to help build his Gifted Team™.

IPS: Hello everybody. I'm thrilled to have a special guest with us on the line today. A lot of you know Shaun Irwin. He has been a member of Quantum Club™ for quite a while now and a Private Client Group member for quite a while now, and he is not shy. So, it's not unlikely that if you've been to a live event that you've seen and heard Shaun before. He's also a very generous contributor, and so you'll often see him making comments on the Qmail discussion group. It's no secret that Shaun was selected by our independent panel of judges to drive my Audi home from the Boot Camp/Summit—he was the final winner of our first Best Year Ever contest. He was also our Marketer of the Year. I have the pleasure of spending some time on the line right now with somebody who has not only made a significant difference to a lot of the businesses and lives of other Quantum Club™ members, but has also demonstrated a personal mastery of a lot of the principles that we teach and talk about. So Shaun, good morning. How are you?

Shaun Irwin: Good morning. Thank you, I'm doing well.

IPS: We have a lot of ground to cover. I want to remind everyone that at the end of my interview and conversation with Shaun, you'll have the opportunity to ask him questions. Shaun, there are a number of things I want to cover, and I know that there are some things that you want to cover during the course of this call. We want to talk about some of the success that you've had in your agency over the last few years. When you and I were preparing for the call yesterday, you had mentioned that you also want to make sure that we cover some of the life changes that you've been able to affect in your life over the last few years and how important that's been to you and Cindy and the family. And we want to make sure that we talk about *some of the ways that you've taken the Quantum Club™ principles and applied them in interesting areas like nurturing your employees and employee retention strategies, as well as nurturing clients and things like that.*

ENTERING THE CONTEST

But, I thought it might be an appropriate place for us to start by talking a little bit about the contest. Obviously you entered the contest and won. I want to encourage people because we now have another contest and car giveaway this year. I wonder if you would share what it was like for you to go through that submission phase. It shows up in the summer where you have to reflect back on the year and identify your successes, both financial and otherwise. What was that experience like for you?

Shaun: I'll preface it by saying I really want to thank you for having me on the call and I want to thank everybody in Quantum Club™ and Private Client Group™ that has helped me along the way. It has been a wonderful experience. When they hand the keys over to an agent when you buy an agency, it doesn't come with a manual. So, it was pretty interesting for me. I bought an agency in 1998, and I believe that I joined Quantum Club™ in 2000. It has been the wealth of information, knowledge and energy from the people involved in Quantum Club™ that has made some of the most significant impact. So, first, I want to make sure I don't forget to say thank you to everyone. The contest itself, interestingly enough—and I put this in my submission—if anybody talked to me or asked me, I would tell them that I really wasn't going to enter the contest. For whatever reason, like I'm busy, I do a lot of things and I spend a lot of energy thinking up new things and challenging my staff and challenging my family and friends to tell me to shut up occasionally and more often than occasionally sometimes.

WORK ON THE BUSINESS

We were in a process meeting one day that I easily could've not been in the room for. I could see around the room the energy and that people got it. So the light went off for me—it had already gone off for them apparently—but for me, that "oh my gosh, it's really working" really translated itself then. A lot of agency owners that I meet, they are the energy and the driving force, and that's not to say that I don't play a valuable role, but if I got out of this process meeting that we were having, it would be better without me there. And, in fact, the following week, that's what they asked me to do. It was the following week or two weeks later they asked me not to come anymore so they could finish their work without me being disruptive, which I occasionally am. I literally was choked up and couldn't really complete what I wanted to say because it was a big, big deal. I sat down and thought, "Well, if that's not the best year ever, then nothing is." So that was when I made the decision to make a submission, and felt worthy, so-to-speak, of making a submission, and then next I had to reflect on what has happened. That was a whole other illuminating experiencing of, "Oh my gosh, we're really doing a lot of stuff." There was a whole list of

> "It has been the wealth of information, knowledge and energy from the people involved in Quantum Club that has made some of the most significant impact."

things that, from when we started with the building blocks of success, that we have added this quarter, or even this month. It just is an additional progressive track that we follow.

IPS: I have two questions for you that came out of that. First, how did you get your agency to the point where the employees did "get it"?

Shaun: I don't know. Maybe I would be you and would be able to sell Quantum Club™ memberships if I knew that. I think certainly it's a matter of believing in myself. I think internally you also have to have a few champions that believe as well and communicate it in a personal sense to a couple of people to help build momentum.

IPS: How do you communicate this stuff to your key people? How did you find your champion?

PARTICIPATORY STAFF

Shaun: Part of it, I will say—and this is a bit of a commercial for you—is the CSR Mastery Program™. We've had our folks involved in the CSR Mastery Program™. For the last four years I've brought people from my agency to the Boot Camps/Summit and have had them participate in the Boot Camp/Summit from a listening standpoint and a developing standpoint. I have them, when we come back, work on various things that they may have learned at Boot Camp/Summit.

IPS: And one of them, I think it was Rebecca, drove the Audi home, didn't she?

Shaun: Well, it is participatory, so she did get to drive that home and reflect on the contest itself this year: I think it built such a huge amount of excitement that I don't know how anyone can miss it next year. And this isn't just because I was involved. Had I not won, it would've been just as exciting—it was really something.

THE ZONE OF TOTAL CONFIDENCE™

IPS: Okay, my second question then Shaun is briefly, for those that don't know you as well, how would you describe the difference between your agency now and your agency four or five years ago?

Shaun: What types of changes are you looking for?

IPS: More money, more control, more time off. I think one of things that is striking about your experience, for those of us who know you, is we'd say that now Shaun has entered into the Zone of Total Confidence™. You know that you can take increasingly long periods of time away from the agency, which you do. And you can do it with the confidence that when you come back, it'll probably be bigger than when you left and it'll run smoothly. You can really devote the energy and attention in your life to things that you care about.

Shaun: And work on other things and be involved in the community. There is a whole list of advantages that go with that.

IPS: One of the four elements of what we call the Zone of Total Confidence™ is whether you can start more businesses in or outside of the industry if you want to. You've been able to do that as well.

Shaun: Correct. We have three different businesses going at the same time, and we're involved in the aspects of those businesses that I enjoy. In other words, I help them with marketing.

IPS: So you're the marketing guy?

Shaun: Well, I'm not the marketing guy because I don't want to go to work there every day. This way, I still get to be involved in some of the things that I have a passion for in those businesses, but I don't have to do all of the everyday stuff. The businesses are completely unrelated, by the way. One is healthcare, one is manufacturing, and one is semi-related to the insurance business, but the other two could not be more different from insurance.

EXECUTING AND IMPLEMENTING

IPS: Shaun, you're going to be at the Closed Door conference. I had asked you yesterday if you were going to be there, would you be willing to give a short presentation. I wasn't surprised that you said you were going to be there because you make it a habit to participate. I think that one of the things that strikes me about my observation of you is that when there is an opportunity, whatever it is, you execute. You don't hold back. And I'm assuming that that's sort of a characteristic of Shaun regardless of Quantum Club™ participation, you'd be implementing.

Shaun: I guess the question would be what would I be implementing? There are so many tools that have been added to my arsenal. I would be doing something. Again, people who know me would describe me as somebody who can't sit still. I would be described as somebody who has made the entrepreneurial ADD that we talk about. I had a marketing meeting a week and a half ago, and somebody said, "Well, why do we do all this different stuff?" And I said, "Well, I'd get bored if we didn't." Their point was maybe we just want to focus on one thing for a while. And maybe we should, but it wouldn't be as much fun for me to just focus on one thing and one thing only. So, that's me, and that's part of figuring out your gift and your business

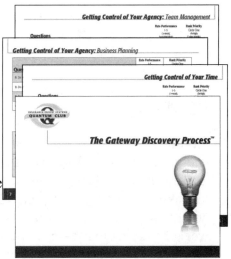

model, and deciding what you want it to look like. There are people who have made a fortune selling high-risk auto insurance. I don't like it. So, that's not what I'm going to do. It doesn't mean there's anything fundamentally flawed with their model. In fact, it can be a great model. I know people that have done very well and enjoy it, but that's not my model. That is just something that each person needs to answer for him or herself.

PLANNING TOOLS

I have said for people like me, with the Quick Start mentality—and I know there are a lot of us in Quantum

Club™—that it is so important to use the planning tools that we have access to through Quantum Club™. Things like the Gateway Discovery Process™, and Quarterly Planning, they help quiet my mind and keep it from going in 83 different directions, and point me in the right direction. The person who pointed me downhill in the first place, who I have to give credit to, is my daughter, who is now 10 years old. She was four years old right before I joined Quantum Club™. We were talking about the family going somewhere and doing something, and she said that mom, Patrick, and her will go somewhere. And I said, "What about me?"

IPS: *How old is Patrick?*

Shaun: He is 12 now, so he was six then. Kelly, my daughter, was four. This was a couple months before joining Quantum Club™, and it was one thing that led up to making the decision to join. Kelly said, "Mom, Patrick, and I will go" to whatever it was, something fun on the weekend, going to Mall of America or something like that. And I said, "Well, what about me? Maybe Dad would want to go." And she said, "Well, you'll be working." I said, "What do you mean I'll be working?" She said, "Well, you always work, Dad." They don't lie when they're four. She didn't say it in a negative or judgmental way. It was just a fact. "You'll be working." And I did at the time. I worked a lot. Then, I channeled my energy in a different way. I worked on the weekends, on some marketing or whatever it was. What happened—for me, at least—is if I did that, I did not disengage my mind from it the whole weekend. Maybe I only worked for two or three hours in my office at home, but I didn't shift and I didn't completely turn that off after I stopped working. So I made a little goal for that summer that I would try to take every weekend off. And I was able to do it. So, now that's what I do. Now you will see me at a Quantum Club™ thing, but if I'm in town, I really don't work on the weekends. I really don't. Now what I'm trying to accomplish is the prioritization. What comes first, what comes second? Is your business a business, or is it your life?

THE TRUE NORTH COMPASS™

IPS: *In your official submission form, you referenced the True North Values Compass™. Did that help clarify those priorities for you?*

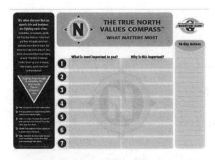

Shaun: Very much so. I was on a nonprofit board and I have always known that we have been given so many gifts and so many blessings, so fundamentally I understood that. But I have a much more thoughtful approach now. I'm at my kid's ballgames. We coach whatever sport they'll let us. Patrick is 12, so they're getting a little beyond my capability—now they're better than I am at the sports that they're playing. But the point is I'm involved. I don't miss the dance recital; I don't miss when the kids have a program at school. And I don't work until midnight to make up for it. I have talked to agents who say, "I don't miss that stuff, but I go back to my office and work until midnight." I don't do that anymore. And that has really been a process of thoughtfully prioritizing what is important. Like anyone, it's very easy for me to get caught up in more, more, more at work. Not from a money standpoint, but because I want to do more, I want to build more. I love the puzzle of business.

MARKETING TOOLS

IPS: *Shaun, can we dig into marketing for a minute or two, looking over the past year, The Best Year Ever, or as you call it, The Best Year So Far?*

Shaun: Yep, The Best Year Yet.

IPS: *So looking at that year, what are some of the marketing tools that have been important to you, or what are some of the strategies that have been important to you?*

Shaun: I would 100% say Automated Response Technology is the one I get the most giggles from because it's so inexpensive. When you combine the effectiveness with the cost, it's about as no-brainer as you can have as a nurturing tool. We use ZipDrip™ for our niche marketing when people come into our website. We have niche websites. We have seven or eight right now; I'm not exactly sure.

NICHE MARKETING

IPS: *So, obviously niche marketing is a really important strategy.*

Shaun: Yes. I guess I take that one for granted.

IPS: *I know. A lot of us do. But I think it's a big eye-opener for a lot of people.*

Shaun: And, to reiterate, for those of you who are generalists or think, "How do I get out of this generalist way of thinking?" our agency has been in business since 1927. We were a generalist agency in the past for 70 years. So, look inward. Look at what you have that you're good at. Maybe you only have half a dozen of them. But find something that you and your staff like, enjoy, and are good at, and build off that.

NICHES

IPS: Your agency was around for a long time. You just bought it in '98?

Shaun: Correct.

IPS: Can you give us a glimpse of how much growth you've seen in the last few years?

> "We will end up close to quadruple in size compared to when we purchased."

Shaun: We will end up close to quadruple in size compared to when we purchased.

EMPLOYEE RETENTION STRATEGIES

IPS: Wow, congratulations on that. A couple of things that the panel was really impressed with in your submission were your employee retention strategies and your approach to that, as well as your charitable giving. So, let's take them one at a time.

Shaun: Well for employee retention, I came up with this little doodad that I thought was important because it dealt with incentives and those things. Anybody who was on Qmail this week, I made a little comment on there about it.

I believe that we have a salesperson's mentalities. Not all of us, but agency principals predominantly have a sales mentality. And we're asking the agents, the people with the service mentality, to buy into incentives that are about money. But, for the most part, they're not buying into that. When we've tested them with both Kolbe and Omnia profiles, they are not driven by that money. They are driven by security, comfort, value, and public and private praise. They are driven by something else. Then I took the context of how much it costs to hire an employee. You've done a lot of hiring, what's your estimate that it costs?

THE COST OF HIRING AN EMPLOYEE

IPS: It's expensive. And a lot of the expenses are the soft cost of all the time it takes for you to screen and interview and do second interviews and then the 90 days of orientation and training and lost opportunity. It's really expensive. What I've heard from the HR industry, and I take everything with a grain of salt, is that it costs a company three times as much to replace an employee as their salary. So, if they're a $40,000 person, then the company is losing $120,000, and a lot of it is the lost opportunity and the time wasted, and so on and so forth. I don't know if that's true or not. I just know that it's an awful waste of time sometimes.

Shaun: And you want to go through a thoughtful process and make sure it's somebody that really is going to stick to your company and it's the right hire. So, even conservatively—let's be conservative—I think everyone can agree that it's approximately $7,500 to $10,000 to hire an employee when you start counting in training, hiring, ads, and all that stuff. Well, my thought process was if we have the employees in place that we want, why not nurture them like you would nurture a relationship that you have with a referral source, a circle of influence, or a customer. Because they are going to be the face, the voice, the name, and the contact repeatedly for these very people that we want to retain. I thought a way to broaden that is to not only do it in the workplace, but also in the home. Of course at work you want to reward certain behavior so you have incentives for cross-sell and you have incentives for adding new business. And you want to keep those because they're building blocks for success, and "our next dollar is a good dollar to get," but on a personal level, also do it for their homes. So not only are you nurturing them, you're nurturing their family relationships so that they say, "Wow, that's a heck of a place to work."

EMPLOYEE-CHOSEN CHARITABLE CONTIBUTIONS

What we do is we actually send things to their homes, and what we send varies each month. By the way, we also pick a name each month, and the employees get to contribute anywhere between $2 and $500 to the charity of their choice, depending on the growth of the agency that month.

IPS: *Who makes the contribution?*

Shaun: The agency does, on their behalf.

IPS: *And is that every month?*

Shaun: Every month. So an employee's name gets picked out of a hat. The employee gives everyone else in the agency a tip, and that tip might be, "You can delete e-mails faster by doing this." They give a tip; we give a charitable contribution. They have some great tips, and for the most part I don't know what they're talking about. But they use them. Again, it's their idea, it's their formulating, and that's in the office, in a public forum. They get to talk about their charity that we're giving it to and why they picked them if they'd like to. Some of them really enjoy that. Bear in mind that these employees that you have, they are rarely writing checks of $500 to a charity in one pop. It's a big deal.

EMPLOYEE NURTURING

We also have what we call a collage of giving, which is essentially a display of the logos of our various charities that we contribute to. We have those in our lobby in a framed plaque. In January we sent that collage of giving to their homes with a certificate behind it that they could then give an additional $50 to the charity of their choice. So that's how it started out. And then we had it easy for February, since Valentine's Day is in February. We love our employees, so we give them a spa certificate. I'm Irish, so in March we have to have St. Patty's Day.

IPS: So, what might show up at their home around St. Patty's Day?

Shaun: A certificate for an Irish pub so they can go and have a meal there.

IPS: Enough so they can take their spouse?

Shaun: Sometimes it is, sometimes it isn't. There are varying amounts. That one wasn't really that big a deal; it was like $15. The one before was more. I think the one for the spa was $50 or $75 on a spa certificate. It just depends on the month. I also put together some copy on one sheet, maybe little poems. I know that people speculate on who writes them, which is kind of fun. They speculate that I don't do that. They think Cindy does. Because they don't think I can write a poem.

IPS: Well, I'm shocked. And what about April?

Shaun: Something to do with flowers. But we have one each and every month.

IPS: Do they come to expect it?

Shaun: That's why we send it at different times.

IPS: So, it's still appreciated. It's been a couple of years since you've been doing this, right?

Shaun: The charitable piece that we do on a monthly basis has been three years. This, to their homes, this is the first year we did that.

HOLIDAY PARTY

We did other things relative to that, which were holidays. Instead of giving holiday bonus checks, I actually go and buy—now I don't go anymore, we buy it on the Internet—but we buy electronics, vacations, things like that. And then we put them in blind envelopes, and they draw them at the holiday party.

IPS: So what might they get?

Shaun: Well, one was a vacation to anywhere in the country they wanted to go, airline tickets and hotel; a digital camcorder; DVD players.

IPS: *So these are kind of serious gifts, aren't they?*

Shaun: Yeah. It's usually $3,000 to $4,000 worth of stuff.

IPS: *Spread among how many?*

Shaun: Right now we have 18. That sounds like a lot of money, but if go back and put it in context of how much it costs to hire an employee, it doesn't seem like so much.

IPS: *Right.*

Shaun: You look at that nurturing and you say, "What's your ROI?" It's a little harder to measure, but retention of employees is pretty damn important.

IPS: *Have you gotten feedback from family members or spouses of the employees about this?*

Shaun: Oh yeah. We get thank you notes all the time. We get them in our home. What's interesting to me is that they've reversed it now. So they're starting to nurture me at home. Like on Boss's Day, I received a card and a gift certificate at my home as opposed to them just slapping it on my desk.

CHARITABLE CONTRIBUTIONS AND NURTURING STRATEGIES

IPS: *You have other charitable activities as well, or charitable contributions besides the ones you make on behalf of employees, right?*

Shaun Irwin: Oh, yes.

IPS: *I'm assuming that's an important part of your agency's orientation, or Shaun's orientation—I'm not sure where you draw the line.*

Shaun: Absolutely. And I'll tell you about one of our nurturing strategies, which in fact is right in line with me and what I care about so that's why I glommed onto it. At some point back when I first joined Quantum Club™, I went to a meeting and a guest speaker talked about the halo effect of charitable marketing or charitable giving. Well, for a segment of our clients, on a quarterly basis we deliver cookies from a nonprofit cookie bakery in North Minneapolis. It's an employment program for disadvantaged youth.

IPS: *So, you make charitable contribution to this nonprofit cookie bakery, and then they make the delivery. Is that how it works?*

Shaun: Well we actually buy them. But as opposed to buying them from a for-profit bakery—which we could do that and deliver them too—we actually buy them from a nonprofit bakery. And then my staff delivers them to our customers. We prominently display that it's this nonprofit and articulate their mission as well.

> "At some point back when I first joined Quantum Club, I went to a meeting and a guest speaker talked about the halo effect of charitable marketing or charitable giving…on a quarterly basis we deliver cookies from a nonprofit bakery."

COMMUNITY SPOTLIGHT

Additionally, in our newsletter, we have a community spotlight where we focus on a nonprofit in each and every newsletter. And they're usually charitable organizations that we give to.

> "They've seen where change can be very positive. It's interesting that you and I are having this discussion because on another level we're having a discussion about how to continue to improve. And I think that's a broader discussion for Quantum Club™ and for Private Client Group™."

IPS: *Got it. Do you write that?*

Shaun: No, I don't write it. We just get information from them and then just cut and paste it. Essentially, what we'll mostly articulate is their mission. And they usually have that down pretty well, so there's no reason for us to write something different. We put their logo, so they get their logo and their branding, if you will. And we care about it. They're organizations that we care about. They're ones our employees care about, or they wouldn't be included in our charitable giving.

IPS: *How often does your newsletter go out?*

Shaun: Oh, whenever we publish it. We have multiple newsletters, because we have niche newsletters as well, so they go out at different times.

ANNUAL STAFF RETREATS

IPS: Your annual staff retreats have become an important ritual as well. You do that once a year, right?

Shaun: Yes, annually.

IPS: How long have you been doing that, and can you tell us what the format of it is?

Shaun: Three years. We do it on Columbus Day. That's intentional because people think of our industry as mostly tied to the financial services and bank industry. Banks are closed on Columbus Day.

IPS: So, it's okay if you're out that day. It's acceptable in your marketplace. And now, what's the purpose of your retreat?

Shaun: The purpose of our retreat is to plan for the coming year. The big topic of discussion at our first one was client segmentation. So you might take a broader topic that you really want to supercharge. I finally resolved, "Okay. We've been talking about this. This is going to happen. We're not going to stop until this happens." And then in terms of format, in the afternoon, we bring in a speaker that talks about a topic that's relevant to facilitating where we want to go. So, for the first two years, our topic really was change.

IPS: Do you select the agenda?

Shaun: Yeah.

IPS: Do you take everybody or just leadership?

Shaun: Everybody.

IPS: Is your purpose to come out with an action plan or is it focusing more on involving people, developing a culture and a philosophy, and the action plan comes later? How far do you think you can get in your one day?

Shaun: For our first one, it definitely was to develop an action plan, but it also was letting people feel better, safer if you will, about the changes that were coming and the changes that continue to come. Remembering now we are primarily a commercial lines agency, and we started doing this at a time of a lot of market upheaval and people having challenging conversations and experiencing process changes internally. The backdrop is, "What if you test these people out, what is their security?" It goes against some of the very things they hold dearly as values. So, how do you make that a more comfortable process for them? You're saying really, "How do you get them to buy in to your vision?" Well, you get that buy in maybe from a different voice than me. And that's where we brought in a professional speaker. This time, our professional speaker that we just had was on decision-making, because now we're a little bit beyond just talking about change. They've gotten there. They've seen where change can be very positive. It's interesting that you and I are having this discussion because on another level we're having a discussion about how to continue to improve. And I think that's a broader discussion for Quantum Club™ and for Private Client Group™.

IPS: *In Private Client Group, as you know, we're focusing a portion of our next meeting on how to run a staff retreat that's effective, involves people, and moves an agency in the direction that you want to go. So, I think that from that we'll be able to develop some tools and training for everybody in Quantum Club™. I'm excited about it because that's a heartbeat of our company. We do quarterly retreats. We do a two-day annual retreat, and then throughout the year we're gathering quarterly retreats and then throughout the entire year we have team meetings that are implementing the objectives and goals that are established at the retreats.*

TEAM MEMBER ROADMAP™

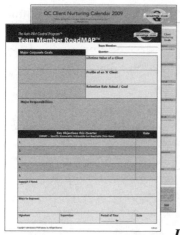

Shaun: Well we use Team Member ROADMAP™. I have to thank Sean McCreary for getting me off my duff on doing those. He embraced that as his strategy, and it works so effectively for him that I made sure we started it too. That has really facilitated remarkable positive change.

IPS: *Shaun, when I walked in our office yesterday, right there at the front desk was a great big stack of* <u>*Client Nurturing Calendars,*</u> *which we're sending everybody. That probably will go in the mail this week. Of course, it's got the stickers for ZipDrip™ and ART and all that kind of stuff.*

CLIENT SEGMENTATION

Specifically, though, a few minutes ago, you referenced client segmentation and how you can't treat every segment the same. If you're going to have VIPs, they have to be treated like VIPs. After you got through that client segmentation exercise three years ago, what did you do differently than you did before?

Shaun: We changed our nurturing calendars. Or I should say we developed nurturing calendars. And I wouldn't say we're that different than a lot of agencies. It wasn't that we didn't send our top clients cookies at the holidays. Again, it just became more thoughtful. It became more pointed. It became more strategic. We went back to that and said, "Okay. What do you do with the A, AA, and AAA? You have those different client sets, what do you do differently?" And I think that gave us good groundwork then to develop those calendars in such a way that they were more meaningful.

IPS: *Shaun, in a moment, I want to be able to open it up for questions. Before we do that, though, let's look back. Obviously, you had a great year. You've had a great run for a number of years. Is there any big thing that you'd pass on to other people who are listening, maybe some who are kind of new to this stuff and some who have been around for awhile and might be missing something? What are the big rocks that you put in the jar first?*

Shaun: Don't be afraid. Execute. The biggest thing is to find one thing you can do and then do it. And then find the number two thing and do that too. And find number three and so on. But just start with one thing.

IPS: Great. Well one of the things that struck me as really interesting is that among the top 10 finalists for the Best Year Ever contest, those are 10 people that I happen to see all the time because they're always showing up at Closed Door conferences and Boot Camps/Summit. They're always participating, and I thought, "That's not a coincidence, is it." So I want to encourage people to do that. I also wanted to announce to people that we are sending a new tool in the mail. We have shared it with Private Client Group before, but have never shared it with Quantum Club™. It's called the Great Idea Filter™. Shaun mentioned the strategy of "find a big thing, do it, and then find the next big thing and do it." The Great Idea Filter™ is intended to help you do that.

> "Don't be afraid. Execute. The biggest thing is to find one thing you can do and then do it. And then find the number two thing and do that too. And find number three and so on. But just start with one thing."

I think we all have more opportunities than time, and the more successful you become, I've noticed that that's even truer. The opportunities are almost thrown at you. I think you develop a mindset to see opportunities that maybe you hadn't seen before. So the Great Idea Filter™ is a tool to help us make strategic decisions about what the best ideas are, which allows us to <u>really work on the big stuff and not be distracted by other things,</u> not waste time on things that are not going to be as productive. Our first caller is Bill.

Bill: Hello, it's great to talk to you today. Wow. Shaun, congratulations first of all for being a winner of the top 10, and I'm sure you're enjoying driving your new Audi TT.

THE AUDI

Shaun: Actually, I will share on this call, and we'll put pictures up later, that I sold the car. So far, I have a Fender Stevie Ray Vaughan Stratocaster and we're redoing our plasma television flat screen living room entertainment center.

Bill: Well I just had a comment. I have three pages of notes here. I can't wait to start all over again and look at these, but Shaun, one of the things that really impressed me is your sincere heartfelt appreciation for what your team is doing in your agency. And obviously, you're rewarding with not only gifts but also gratitude and concern. That's coming through, and I'll tell you what, I'm envious. I have a great team, and we're going to have our Christmas party tonight, and I think I'll order extra desserts for them. I think one thing that helps your agency be a complete agency is to have that team well oiled and to reward them for what they do and to let them know that you appreciate it, and I thank you for sharing that.

Shaun: I will add one thing. And it's not to say that I'm not demanding, because I am. I want us to be the best, and I truly want that for myself and I truly want that for them. I truly want them to live their dreams, but if I'm going to have high expectations, then I have to treat them with high regard.

IPS: I also have pages of notes myself, Shaun. There's a lot. I never stop learning from people in Quantum Club™, so I appreciate everything that you've shared today. Shaun, have a terrific day. As always, I appreciate your generosity and as always, congratulations on the successes that you've had and the way that you shared them with people around you, both family and community and us. Thanks a lot.

"Michael...thanks for: Life: more time off (5 weeks) than ever to experience magical moments with my family/friends. Business: increased net income by $100K using HIM(high-impact marketing). It all came from my existing clients! Quantum Club: the ultimate brain trust! Nowhere else can you get the trusted insights of America's savviest insurance agents. Thanks a million for giving us each other!"
~Sean McCreary, Tracy, California

"Once again I learned new things that will help me make money and get more control of my time. Thanks for what you do! Michael, by just implementing a couple of the things you teach we had a 49.5% increase in commissions and 139% increase in profits. In 2008, added another 43% to our bottom line, boosted top line another 20%. Took 5 weeks of vacation and never called the office."
~Chet Cottom, Claremore, OK

"I have learned little things each time that have made thousands of dollars, saved me thousands of dollars and help grow my agency 35% per year. With your tools and the things I learned from you, income is up 52% and profit is up 78% from 1 year ago."
~Don Dahlmeier, Chico, CA

Lee Hendrie: Commercial & Personal lines in California

Lee Hendrie, a long time Quantum Club™ member continues to grow his agency. He averages over 238 new personal lines accounts a month and 37 new commercial accounts per month. He's an Agency Mastery Program™ Coach and he is a Mastery Agency Principal in his own right. He's got a great reputation. He's been doing this for a few years. He grew up with a father who owned a small insurance agency in Michigan and after graduating from college with a degree in insurance he came home to his father saying "I told you I was selling the agency, so go start your own." He now runs a very formidable agency with over four-million in income and he still manages to take over 26-weeks a year off.

IPS: We have today Lee Hendrie. For those of you who don't know Lee, sorry for you, because he's got a wealth of knowledge and wisdom. Lee has been a Quantum Club™ member for…Lee, how long?

Lee Hendrie: About four years.

IPS: Oh, four years. He's an Agency Mastery Program™ Coach and he is a Master Agency Principal in his own right. He's been doing this for a few years. He runs a very formidable agency. He's got a great reputation and his agency continues to grow. So, let me start by introducing Lee. How are you Lee?

Lee: Well, I'm doing just fine. How are you Michael?

IPS: I'm doing fantastic, thank you.

Lee: Good.

IPS: Let's start by giving people an opportunity to get to know you a little bit. You've got a great story and so why don't we start with a little bit of background on who Lee Hendrie is and how you got to be where you are today.

Lee: Well Michael, I actually grew up around the insurance business. My Dad had a very small agency in Michigan and I thought this would be a great business. He was respected in the community and it looked like a clean business and like he was having a lot of fun. So I thought this would be the way to do it, so I went to college – Michigan State – and I got a degree in insurance and then I thought I would go back and help my Dad and he said, "I told you I was selling the agency, so go start your own." So I said, "Okay." So I went to Travelers because I wanted

to get hired, because I didn't know exactly how to go about this and I ended up in the Fidelity Surety Department in Los Angeles. So I learned how to be a Fidelity Insurance person and so that's basically the banking end of insurance and I did just about every conceivable thing, so after I'd been there six years I decided I'll try the Life business, because if I could learn how to sell, then maybe I could do my Property & Casualty. So I spent a couple years there and got my CLU and I was able to survive in Life only, so I decided to move to Orange County where I knew nobody and I started my agency. I built it up to seven offices – 6 in California, statewide, and 1 over in Scottsdale, Arizona. And then I thought, well, you know, I think I'll retire at 53, so I did. I sold the business to two people that worked for me who were excellent insurance men and I kept the stock until they could pay it off. And as it turned out, they weren't able to run it as a business. And so I got a call to come back and take it back, so I did. And we had been reduced down to one office and very few employees and about 25% of the income, and a seven-figure debt.
So I got busy and started working again, which was probably what I needed all along.

$4 MILLION IN INCOME

IPS: *I can't imagine you not working.*

Lee: So anyway, I got busy and started doing this thing and I had built it back up to three offices and the income now exceeds what I left it with, although they're today's dollars compared to 1990 dollars.

IPS: *But gosh, it still is over four-million dollars in income.*

Lee: Yeah, right, it's still over four-million in income.

IPS: Okay. I guess I was teasing you about never imagining you not working, because I think you enjoy it a lot, but you do get a little bit of free time, don't you?

Lee: Yes, I take 26-weeks a year off and I'm able to do that because we have a great team, very good leaders, in fact this next staff meeting is my staff appreciation meeting and we have done nothing but nurture them, as well as our customers.

> "I got busy and started doing this thing and I had built it back up to three offices and the income now exceeds what I left with…it's over four-million in income."

IPS: Right. Okay. And you've got marketing that's on a RAM cycle, so it reliably runs itself even when you're on one of your 26 weeks of vacation.

Lee: Absolutely. It keeps growing. Last year we averaged 238 new personal lines accounts a month and we averaged 37 new commercial accounts.

IPS: Alright! And a lot of people are kind of whining that business is slow or down or new apps are down because of soft market or conversions down, but you had 238 new accounts…

Lee: Yes. Right.

IPS: …per month last year.

Lee: Right.

IPS: *Alright. And so that's down a little for you, because it was down 11 from the previous year.*

Lee: Right, we had roughly 250, with a soft market, of course that makes it a little more difficult, but there are so many people and if you've got any kind of a service organization and referral program, those types of things should never stop you from continuing to write business.

THE REAL MEAT AND POTATOES

IPS: *Alright. So, I promised that we would deliver some real meat and potatoes on how it is you became as successful as you are and really dive into some of the things that are working. I also wanted to mention that you've got a very respectable retention rate – 93.7% on personal lines.*

Lee: Yeah. Let me just tell you about the last 5 years. I did take the time to look at my retention numbers and of course the first time I heard about an Easy Millions Spreadsheet, I looked at it and I said, "Gee, it makes sense to go after retaining the business." So in the first year, we had 9,154 renewals, but just remember 9,000. And we did 90.0% retention that year. And then the following year, it went up to 90.8% on about 12,700 renewals. Then it went up to 91.5% and we had 15,752 renewals. In the next year it jumped to 92.3% and then it went up to 17,738 and finally it jumped to 93.4% with 18,918 renewals. This is just the personal lines.

IPS: *How many renewals that year?*

Lee: 18,918, so basically we went from 9,000 to 19,000 in five years, as far as renewals and personal lines.

IPS: And your retention went from 90% to 93.4%.

Lee: Right. And so far this year it's 93.7%. The commercial renews at the rate of 96% and in the first year, because I had to buy back the stock of the two people that I had sold the business to, I started with a zero commercial department and zero companies basically. We are now writing about $5-million in premium with about a $750,000 income and we write less than 1% of it in Workers Comp, so that's why we get a little bit better income percentage. So that's kind of like a growth in retention figure for both departments.

> "We went from 9,000 to 19,000 in five years as far as renewals and personal lines...retention went from 90% to 93.4%"

IPS: So that was zero in the first year?

Lee: Yes, now we're writing about $5-million, so that's about $1- million a year in commercial premium, so I talk commissions mostly just because I can't spend the premiums, or at least you're not supposed to.

IPS: We'd all prefer it if you didn't. So, you know, I scribbled down these numbers that you threw at us here in terms of your ever-increasing retention rate and I guess there is a lesson in there for all of us, because I know you're very disciplined with the use of the nurturing tools and strategies. You're saying they WORK!

NURTURING YOUR CLIENTS REALLY WORKS

Lee: That's absolutely true.

IPS: *Alright. For example: the newsletter – a lot of people think, "I can't afford to send a newsletter out. It's too expensive." You're sending out how many newsletters?*

Lee: We're sending out about 12,000 newsletters a month.

IPS: *12,000 a month?*

Lee: Right. And we have our own mailing equipment and we have the smart program where they keep the addresses up to date and so forth. And that equipment originally cost about $26,000 and last year alone we saved over $26,000 in postage, it's like investing to make money and you can put it on payments, pay it off and you're so far ahead it's unbelievable.

> "More and more of our members are seeing what happens to your retention and your cross-selling and referrals with a solid newsletter program."

IPS: *Okay, very good. IPS also provides newsletter content through our AMD Program or Automatic Marketing Department™.*

Lee: That's a good thing.

IPS: Well, so many people said they really wanted to do newsletters. More and more of our members are seeing what happens to your retention and your cross-selling and referrals with a solid newsletter program. I think we've hit a critical mass, so I am curious if you've run the Easy Millions™ Spreadsheet on it...you've almost got an extra 4 points of retention.

Lee: Right. And that's equivalent to over $3-million ...

IPS: $3,000,000.00

Lee: Over the 10-year period.

IPS: Okay. So, I guess it's worth sending out a newsletter once in awhile, huh?

Lee: Well, it certainly pays for itself and it also helps the referral business and every other part of the total program of how you get new business.

IPS: Are you getting a lot of referrals?

REFERRALS: THE BACKBONE OF BUSINESS

Lee: We write about 43% of our business as referrals and we get those from centers of influence. We get them from mortgage bankers, real estate agents. Anyway, all the people that deal with people when they buy and sell things. I've got a new program that I'm going to be niching – the high-value home, which is people that have multi-million dollar houses and so forth. We are going to send out mailers to get more of those types of people. We're sending to financial planners, attorneys that handle trusts and estates, that make up trusts, very high-end real estate agents - let's say somebody in a Beverly Hills area for example – that just sell multi-million dollar houses; Business managers for high paid people like sports figures, movie figures, even politicians. In fact, Trent Lott, as some of you might have noted in that *National Underwriter,* had he talked to an insurance agent, he wouldn't have had the problems that he had with State Farm and his vindictiveness now towards our business.

> "We write about 43% of our business as referrals and we get those from centers of influence. We get them from mortgage bankers, real estate agents. Anyway, all the people that deal with people when they buy and sell things."

IPS: *Now he's threatening the entire industry. We should all be watching that very carefully.*

Lee: Right. And then there are bank professionals and accountants that handle these types of people.

IPS: *Family offices if you've got those in that area.*

Lee: Which ones?

IPS: *Family offices – people who sort of manage very, very wealthy families.*

Lee: So I would recommend people expand their centers of influence, because you cannot do it one-on-one. The tools that we have at IPS are helpful, but don't overlook getting that center of influence, because you have to have people working for you free.

IPS: Do you put centers of influence on your newsletter mailing list?

Lee: Ah, yes.

IPS: Okay.

Lee: I try to send it out to everybody that will take it.

COMMERCIAL LINE GROWTH

IPS: Yes. Alright. Everybody?

Lee: We try. We have about 3,000 to 4,000 e-mail addresses, so we do some of it by e-mail.

IPS: Uh-huh. Got it. Alright. So let's step back. I wanted to look at the growth of your commercial lines business. You've grown from zero to about a million a year in new commercial lines business and I know that you've niched it with your apartments. And condos?

Lee: We have condos. We have property owners. We have restaurants and now we're doing the high-value type customer and the apartments – see, we've always been a strong property agency and very low on Workers Comp. California has a tendency to make that an extremely volatile line and I saw a lot of my people go out of business when they had open ratings come in, so I never really paid much attention to that, but I've loved to write buildings, strip centers, all types of apartments, condominiums and those things are low maintenance, which cuts down on your staffing needs. It's low loss-ratio type business and so contingencies are up and you can negotiate better contracts and higher commissions. Russ has already mentioned that, you know, like one of the companies that he and I both represent pays 20%. And I've got others paying 18%. People love property business. I've got one company, which is kind of unusual, but I get 24% from them. And so, you know, you start putting that together, you don't really need to take on that high-maintenance stuff that costs you money. Of course, I'm in it for profit. I'm sorry. I failed to mention that.

IPS: Alright. So give us a sense of how much new business you're writing in that niche.

[handwritten note: Goals for New Acct]

Lee: The apartments: we're averaging about 25 buildings a month. And our building owners: we write about 10 a month. And those are our two key ones. I'm anticipating these high-value homes. My goal, as low as it sounds, is about 2 a month. I'd like to work that up to 1 a week or 4 a month. Now, you may say, "Gee, how come so little?" Those average premiums are $7800 and the ones that really have the assets, those premiums can run $15K-$20K for a personal account. We're establishing a special unit for that and training the sales person. We'll have a separate CSR that will be trained for nothing but high-end type customers and those are different. And so you have to assure your center of influence – take a business manager, for example – that they will not be embarrassed when you handle the account. Plus, when those people call in we'll have them profiled and their names available to our receptionist so she can say, "Yes Sir, Mr. Smith, Nellie's available for the service or Mary Ann is available for the sale." And those people that service those accounts have to know the account.

COLOR VS. BLACK & WHITE

IPS: *Right.*

Lee: So, it's a different thing, so if you get into that area, be sure to work it through. I've been spending about four months and I plan on kicking it off in two more months.

IPS: *Alright. Lee, how are you getting the 25…it's really about 35 or plus in that whole niche of apartments and buildings and property owners? How are you getting those?*

Lee: We have a flyer that we send out and it is in color. And we have a 5" x 7" postcard that we do. And I've read that you have to mail about 7 or 8 times before the person recognizes you. And so I continue to mail and the people accumulate these on their desks and so forth and if their expiration date isn't what I think it is, then they manage to hang on to those and call you. And so we do it primarily with a flyer. Now the reason I use color, and you should get to know how color is used – you know each color means something in marketing. Just go online and it'll show you exactly what the red means and what the green means and the light blue means and what the dark blue means and so forth. And it will improve your retention, because about 65% of the people will look at a colored flyer versus a black and

> "…it will improve your retention, because about 65% of the people will look at a colored flyer versus a black and white flyer, about 17% read those."

white flyer, about 17% read those. So, you know, those are things that make that little bit of difference when sending out your mailings.

IPS: *How many flyers do you mail? For flyers or postcards, what's your monthly mailing for that niche?*

Lee: Well, we do about 10K apartments. We do about 10K to building owners. And we do that every single month. And of course I realize I'm in Southern California, so we have a lot of apartment buildings, but have it broken down into three categories for both Orange County and LA County. We have small, medium and large, so to speak. If it's fewer than five, our personal lines handle it. And then we have 5 to 20 units or 'doors' as they call them. Or above 20 and we attacked each one on that basis.

IPS: *Do they get a different flyer?*

Lee: No, we have them broken down as far as comparative rates, you know, what we can do for them and we have them in those three categories, but when we do our mailings, we actually mail to those three categories separately, just for our own internal use.

IPS: *Okay. Now, what do you think your unique selling proposition is?*

THE UNIQUE SELLING PROPOSITION

Lee: Actually, that one, both of those are sold as much on price as they are on anything else. I will tell you Michael, that after 3 years and a half, 3-1/2 roughly, I finally came up with a USP for my agency and I got that after our meeting down in San Diego in January. I was headed home and I said, "Oh my gosh! I have it!" And so, of course our name is Ph.D, but it's "Dependability in an uncertain insurance world" and that's in parentheses and it's on our stationery; we revised our brochure. We revised everything; everything that goes out of there now has our USP for the agency. And we do come up with USP's for our marketing programs and they are so hard to do.

IPS: *Well though, in this niche, the reason people call is it largely because there is an attractive price offer?*

Lee: There is an attractive price offer and of course the piece is very attractive.

IPS: *I haven't seen this flyer, so I'm always curious what the hook is, so…*

Lee: Well, what I should do is, you know if I knew how to upload and download and all that stuff, I'll try to get my commercial guy to do it.
 I mean I'm just not good at that, but…

IPS: *We can get it on the library or you can get it to me to critique.*

Lee: Yeah, okay.

IPS: *Okay.*

Lee: Would you like me to just basically state how in the heck do you get started in marketing? Because I basically took all the things that I read about you and heard from you and I kind of put together a list that I would be glad to provide anybody, because I actually typed it up.

IPS: Absolutely! Yeh, of course.

Lee: So, first of all, I did what everybody does when they come into IPS or at least a good portion of us. I took our little profit circle and I jumped right over there to marketing and found out that that was the wrong direction and I've heard other people say that. So I finally went back to the first little thing – time management – and said, "What am I doing?"

IPS: Yeh, okay.

Lee: So I spent one week auditing every single thing that I did and what I spent time on and of course I used the Mad Dog Time Optimizer™. In fact I told you I was having a hard time even using that, but I've started to eliminate things that I shouldn't be doing and then I delegated tons and tons and tons of stuff. I think that 5% became almost 50% and I developed my sheet, you know, "What Not to Do", because that seemed like it was longer than what I should be doing.

ELIMINATE AND DELEGATE AND CONTROL YOUR TIME

So then after you eliminate and delegate and find out how in the heck you can control your time, I had to decide on what would make the most difference in how we attracted people and of course that answer is the high-impact marketing and actually building business systems. And so I started reading and studying and doing all these things that you said. In fact, just this morning I was back looking in - coming up with a list of all the media that I should make available and I was finally smart enough to type it in my computer this morning, because I remembered, "Gosh, there's 30 different ways that I know I should be using media and I'm not using them all, so let's see what they were." And it took me awhile to find it, but I knew it was in the "All Beef™ Newsletter" thing and I keep all those.

So then after I, you know, figured it out – high impact marketing like I said – I committed to learning the marketing, so I went out after testimonials and it was very important that you set up samples to help your clients. I went to my really good clients first and you know they would sign anything but maybe not the check, but they did everything else and this has been very important to get the testimonials. We now have about four books with probably over a thousand in each book and we have them broken down by CSR. We have them broken down by sales people. We have them broken down by office. We have them broken down by, you know, whatever type of experience they had. And so we got claims. We got service. We got sales. We got all kinds of them. So we can pull those out, because we got them so organized to help us in our various marketing campaigns.

So then I did start the niching and I got to remind everybody that you've got to test the postcards, the sales letters, the newspaper ads, the newspaper inserts, yellow pages, e-mails, Post-It notes, website – I tried them all. I tested them all. Yellow Pages have kind of gone off the charts and I haven't used the Yellow Pages now for quite awhile. And one of the things that a lot of people may not know, but the "Do Not Call List" does not include everybody. There are a lot of names and you can go to the Haines, let's see – the cross directory people – that's Haines isn't it? Yeh, anyway, they can show you which names are on the "Do Not Call List" and those that you can call and that is something that people overlook, because now they think they can't call anybody anymore. And you can if you just know who to call. And then we set up our referral programs and you can probably see everything from getting the centers of influence to like John Mason did

"Quantum Club members have **access to all of the other Members**. Email them, ask questions, form partnerships…capitalize on opportunities together. You CANNOT overestimate the value of learning from your peers."

the emergency contact campaign. There are others that have done it and those are very good. Then we started our publicity and you need to work with that and that's having a regular press release every week or month – whatever you can do to the local press on matters relating to insurance and safety – and there's plenty of material. If you did nothing more than get the book and become the author, you can page through that – you'll never run out of material.

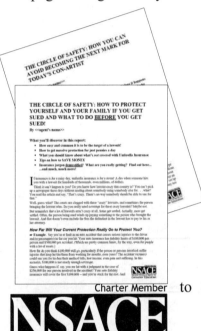

IPS: *The Circle of Safety™.*

Lee: Yeh, *The Circle of Safety™* book that we're allowed to do. Then, of course, I have to remind everybody to do the math and we have done that for years. We call it "Sourcing". And we've got about 24 ways to source. And we trace each lead and sale back to the original advertising source and that will enable you to know "Hey, I need to work more on this one, because it's producing great results." Or you need to kill it. And I've had to kill some and I mean, it kills your ego along with it, but that's okay.

IPS: *When you're in for the profit then that's the ego at least.*

REVENUE PER CLIENT

Lee: And here's one where I see a lot of it currently going on, that's marketing to your existing clients and I think you've kind of pushed that most recently. And you just have to grow the revenue per client and increase the retention and we covered retention, but growing the revenue per customer is so, so important. It's the herd - like Michael has said so many, many times – it's the Herd Concept and you've got to use it.

IPS: Yes. Okay.

Lee: And then we really have a big Nurturing Program, you know, when we contact through the newsletter. We do it through e-mail. We send out hand-written cards. Every single one of our people has to send five cards out, hand-written, to their customer: "Thanks a lot for your business. I just hope everything's going well." - Just a little short note. They only have to do five a week, but of course I've got a lot of employees, so we're sending out maybe 100 of those things…let's see, there's probably 10, 25, 50…yeh, we're probably sending out, well, closer to 200 a month. And those are not designed to sell anything, it's just "Thanks for your business. We've been thinking about you." There are so many members with great ideas – everybody just use them. Geez, I mean, I wasn't smart at all. All I did was look at what everybody else was doing and I thought "Hey, if it worked for him, maybe it'll work for me." And then, like I mentioned, the training and nurturing of your staff – I mean we are really in to it. I know our Unfair Claims Practices training is this next staff meeting. That's required in California. In May, we do our Privacy training. We pay for all the education for our people. They have to have approval of what they do, so they're not just taking Homeowners over and over again, for example. We make them take Umbrella; we make them take other things, so we control their educational system so it's beneficial to the agency. And so those are probably like the ten steps that I think.

IPS: *Got it all - I wrote down ten steps, so I'm glad I didn't miss anything here. So far I've got 3-1/2 pages of notes Lee.*

Lee: Well, I guess I've been verbose.

IPS: *No. I'm learning from one of the Masters. Okay. I do want to see if we've got some questions. Before I open it up, Lee is there anything else that you want to share?*

Lee: Well, all I know is that this is the most exciting business that there is. And if you don't have fun at this business from the moment you get to your shop 'til you leave at night, you're probably not in the right business, because I have never, never had a day where I hated to come to work. It's so important. This is an exciting, dynamic, fun-filled business.

IPS: *Alright. You know, also I wanted to mention to those of you who don't know Lee; Lee's been around for awhile. It's not like he's, kind of just feelin' his way through the beginning of this industry. He's been around. He was successful before he was a Quantum Club™ member and yet, unless he's on one of his 26 weeks of vacation, he participates very actively at every Closed Door*

Conference. He even comes to New Member Orientations. He's always at Boot Camp/Summit. You know, like I said, he's one of our Agency Mastery Program™ Coaches and I think Lee typifies that axiom "School is never out for the pros".

Lee: We've got our company now in its 41st year and you know I just wish I could be here for another 41 years. Of course, I do plan to live to be 110, so I've got 40 left.

QUESTIONS FOR LEE

IPS: Alright, so if anybody's got any questions about anything for Lee, now is your opportunity, otherwise, I don't know Lee, if you're going to be able to join us at the Closed Door Conference in Minneapolis, but this is a rare opportunity for people to talk directly to somebody who is extremely successful.

Lee: Well, I don't know whether or not I'm going to make that one, because that does occur during one of my couple weeks off, but…

IPS: During one of your couple of weeks off.

Lee: But since I'm not going to Washington D.C. for something else I had, I might switch that.

IPS: Okay, well we'd love to see you.

Gary: Good Evening Gentlemen or Good Afternoon Gentlemen. Welcome from beautiful North Carolina.

IPS: Right on. Been there.

Gary: Okay. Great. Lee, I have a question to get more information about your high-valued homeowners program. You mentioned some spheres of influence. Are you going to just work that program through referral or are you going to try and market directly to the homeowners through some color flyer or what-have-you?

Lee: I'm going to do direct marketing to them, as well as through these various types of centers that I had mentioned. I think that, just for your information, that particular market – three-quarters of it is controlled by the direct writers and they are not prepared to do that type of work, so there is a huge, huge market available, because their policies just aren't comprehensive and the main players in that for coverage purposes are AIG, Fireman's Fund, Chubb, and Atlantic Mutual. And so you get the premium product, but yes, Gary, I do plan on mailing direct to them, plus through these other sources. And like I said, my goal is low, but the premiums are high, but I expect to have my four people in that unit within two years.

Gary: Wow! Could you post on the Library, the flyer or whatever media you will use to send directly to those high-value prospects?

Lee: I will when I get it finished. I'm working on it now.

Gary: Okay.

Lee: So I'll get it posted somehow. I'll get somebody who knows how to do it. I'm not very good with the computer.

Gary: Thank you.

Lee: Okay Gary.

IPS: Alright Gary, anything else? Okay.

Bill: How you doing Lee?

Lee: Good. How are you?

Bill: I don't know. Hey, Lee, how long have you been a Quantum Club™ member?

Lee: About 4-1/2 years.

Bill: 4-1/2 years. You know, I was doing the quick math on this, if you'd have been a Quantum Club™ member 9-years, you know with everything you've done, you've probably cost yourself about $5-6 million. You know that don't you?

Lee: Yeh, I know. I wish I would have discovered Quantum Club™ earlier.

Bill: But, hey, I have two quick questions for you and I'll let you get back, but of the 12K newsletters that you're sending out monthly...

Lee: Yes.

> *"I was doing the quick math on this, if you'd have been a Quantum Club member 9-years, you know with everything you've done, you've probably cost yourself about $5-$6 million. You know that don't you?"*

Bill: Can you give me a breakdown on what you're sending to personal line clients, commercial clients, centers of influence, and then also if you're doing a special for realtors or mortgage brokers?

Lee: Well, I can't give you exactly, but it's about 10K that is going to personal lines accounts and then we have about 2K going between commercial and the centers of influence.

Bill: Okay.

Lee: It'd be hard for me to break it down more than that just because somebody else handles that for me.

Bill: I understand - you're a great delegator. I've known you for a few years now and I hope I have the same amount of passion you do when I get ten years from now, much less later on down the road.

Lee: Oh, you will. You're a winner.

Bill: Oh, but now, is it the same newsletter you're doing or are you doing different content for the centers of influence?

> "…We are going to make some revisions in our newsletter and we're going to do like Michael does – feature a commercial account."

Lee: Actually, we're using the same content, but what I do, of course, is sometimes I put a buck slip in there, which is, you know, those little third of a page…

Bill: Sure.

Lee: If I've got somethin' special to say to a particular center of influence type group.

Bill: Got it.

Lee: You need to stick that in there, because they usually read that and then, you know, obviously most of mine are actually reading the newsletter itself. And we are going to make some revisions in our newsletter and we're going to do like Michael does – feature a commercial account. In fact, when I hang up here, I'm calling my account I've had about 35 years. I'm going to make him my first commercial account to recognize, because I think that's pretty great.

Bill: I think that's great too. We just started that as well and the first two people we chose were just tickled pink over it. The other question I wanted to ask you was that you mentioned the color in marketing on the internet, Michael, I think I've seen something on there before, but can you guys redirect me how to find out what these colors mean?

Lee: I can get you the website and I'll e-mail it to you or maybe I can get my guy to post it; I guess since everybody might want to know that.

Bill: Yeah.

Lee: What website is best to go in to, there are two of them? I just don't know, because I have someone else do it, but I know there are two websites and we'll put the one that probably gives you the best information.

Bill: Okay, great.

IPS: Alrighty. Bill, there's only one thing I'm looking for when I'm looking at color, which one makes me the most money.

Bill: Probably green I guess.

[handwritten note: color to stand out in flyer]

IPS: Well, no, there is something about <u>goldenrod,</u> it's still ugly and it still stands out and it still gets attention, but you know, sometimes, you know, color…

Bill: Well, the end result though is green…

IPS: There are a lot of theories and a lot of thoughts about color, the main thing is, which one is going to jump off somebody's desk or off somebody's kitchen table and get read.

Bill: Right.

Lee: See, there's a difference between light blue and dark blue. One of them is the guy that budgets his money and so forth, so he's kind of like the small homeowner type client and if you've got that kind of a list, then you need to use a light blue or a dark blue depending on the type of list you've got. And then <u>red is used sparingly</u> and there's different shades and so forth.

IPS: So, there are some tricks to that. Anything else Bill?

Bill: That's it. Great interview today.

IPS: Yeh, this was fun.

Lee: Thanks Bill.

IPS: Good to hear your voice.

IPS: Hi Roger.

Roger: Hi Lee and Michael.

Lee: Hi Roger.

Roger: Hi, how are you?

Lee: Great. How are you doing?

Roger: Good. I guess what I wanted to find out from you Lee, is what's one of the first things you implemented after joining Quantum Club™, since I just joined recently, just want to kind of get an idea of what one of the first things you implemented.

Lee: Well, I'll tell you what, I went after testimonials first. I mean, I did this eliminate and delegate thing, you know, where I went to marketing and I blew that all to pieces, because I spent a lot of money and got zip, but when I really got started was after I got control of my time. I went after testimonials and I went after them Big Time and you know, I didn't even know what I was doing. I read testimonials on everybody's web pages. I read them in the Library, well they didn't have the Library then, in all Michael's publications and I wrote out so many different ways that you could say the same thing and then I went out and started getting people to do it and of course my staff dragged along 'cuz they thought this was another thirty-day wonder that I was working on. And now they're into it big time.

IPS: 4,000 testimonials later they believe that you're really in to doing this thing?

Lee: Oh, and you know something? Their egos just absolutely get a great boost. In fact, I just got a letter about our service on a guy that was with us ten years and he's leaving and he wrote this fabulous letter telling us what a great organization we are, even though he was leaving. I mean, I'm going to bring it up at my staff meeting a week from Friday and I mean, that's going to go, not in our testimonials, well, kind of like in our testimonials, but it's going to be published by me in some fashion. I haven't decided exactly how to use it, but, it's really worth getting those testimonials.

Paul: Hi Lee. I'm a Captive Agent...how many companies do you sell for?

Lee: Probably I use about 6 or 7 regularly.

Paul: You know, this is kind of personal, but if you had the chance to switch from

> *"...what's one of the first things you implemented after joining Quantum Club...?"*
>
> ~ *"I went after testimonials...."*

being a Captive Agent over to an Independent, what would you be looking for and looking at and what questions would you be asking?

Lee: Well, what I would basically do is look at my own agency and my own personality first to decide: What am I really good at? Then if I was really good at Property, I was really good at Liability, Workers Comp or whatever, then I would go through and I would start looking at the stock companies that had those specialties or even the ones that are the most competitive now, so that when I made the transition and I went to the niche I would have the market that would be priced and have the coverage I was looking for, so getting that appointment would make sense. And, you know, they've got high-impact kits to attract companies, but also, the other thing is when I came back and I had this seven-figure debt, I couldn't show a financial statement. I had zero credibility basically and business. I never transferred over any business and yet you can get markets. So, you pick out the companies you want to go after and if you can't get a direct appointment, a lot of them have managing general agents where you can put the business there until you build the size, you know, enough flow. It doesn't have to be volume – flow – and then go to the company and say, "Look, I'm giving you an average of 10 policies a month or whatever it is, and I'm doing it through this MGA and now I'd like a direct appointment." And that's how you get a company if you were starting out with zero.

Paul: Sure. Hey Michael, does anybody in Quantum Club™ know anything about SIAA?

IPS: Yeah, absolutely. We've got SIAA members and we've got a lot of people that have researched that and similar organizations. My suggestion to you, because I'm not sure who to direct you to, my suggestion to you is that you hop on Q-mail and see if you can get a thread going and some questions going.

Paul: Okay.

IPS: With a subject line that's very clear: Question About SIAA or something like that and then you'll probably get a little bit of response and then you find out if you can network with 2 or 3 of our members who are in it and get the pros and the cons and maybe network with 2 or 3 who chose not to get in it and get the pros and cons and you might find somebody who left it, but within our network I think you're going to find some people that know a lot about what you're talking about.

Lee: Paul, did I give you a good enough answer for that?

Paul: You did, yes you did, you know I've got a lot of homework to do before I make a decision.

IPS: You bet.

Paul: Okay. Thanks guys.

Mark: Saved the best for last.

Lee: Hi Mark. I'm glad you're on.

Mark: Well, how are you guy's doin'?

Lee & IPS: We're doing well.

Lee: Well great. How are you?

Mark: Doin' wonderful. I've got two questions, but first off I'd like to say Lee, you are a great inspiration to me and you make what sometimes seems difficult very simple and so thank you for that. Thank you for sharing that with me.

Lee: Thank you.

Mark: First question, I didn't catch…I've been roaming all over the building listening to you on my headset…what did you say you do, as far as, what do you do as far as your in-house mailing? What do you use, AccuZip or something like that?

Lee: I'm not sure what AccuZip is.

Mark: Well, it sorts out the zip codes and…

Lee: Oh, Smart Mail…

Mark: Yes, Smart Mail

Lee: Yes, we have the Smart Mailer and then it's updated, I think it's monthly they update that disc and there's a small cost to keeping that updated, but it saves you that much in postage and duplication of mailing and all that stuff, so it's easily offset, I mean if you're doing the volume that we do.

Mark: And did you say that you do all your own mailing in-house?

> "You spend money, to make more money. It's the same percentage and we're going to spend…my marketing budget this year is $280K."

Lee: Yes, although some of our printing on our bigger mailings, we have a printer that we have a special deal with where we keep the cost down and so we would have a lot of that printed, but if we had postcards or other types of flyers, we do those in-house and we did take advantage of that Xerox situation and we have two of those Xerox machines and you have to guarantee, I think it's 5K pieces a month or something. We have two and probably could use four, but we don't do that. The other thing I wanted to say is that we don't have an advertising budget. What we do, on average, is spend about 7% of our money in advertising. Well, what we do is, I have my whole budget done, I don't put anything in for marketing. I just start spending and I mean, obviously, you know, I know I don't spend $200K in January, for example, but I just spend it and put more mailings out and put more mailings out and I get more and more income and more and more income and at the end of the year it comes out between 6-7%.

IPS: The more you spend…

Lee: You spend more money, you make more money. It's the same percentage and we're going to spend... my marketing budget this year is $280K.

IPS: That's awesome.

Lee: I mean that's what I'm anticipating we'll spend. I don't put that number in. That's the only number I won't put in my budget.

Mark: Well, as long as the return comes back to you, that's all that matters.

Lee: It will. It will come back.

Mark: Absolutely.

Lee: You've just got to believe.

Mark: I had one other question: do you guys use a comparative rating system, either on personal lines or commercial?

Lee: Yes, we have the FSC system.

Mark: FSC?

Lee: Right and I don't know if they have that out where you are Mark, but there are those rating systems and of course a lot of companies plug in the rates and we're taking this Atlantic Mutual, for example, and I think it's the 12th they'll have the rates on there so we can start finishing up our campaign to kick off, hopefully by June 1st.

Mark: Do you have it on commercial as well?

Lee: We have the availability of it. I don't think we use it a lot. I think most of the rating we do there is directly with the company rating systems, which seem to be friendly, but I'm not sure of that, I think we use the FSCII for some of that commercial.

Mark: Okay.

Lee: We use a lot of direct sites with the companies.

Mark: Okay. Well thanks.

Lee: Was that helpful?

Mark: Yes, absolutely.

Lee: Okay Mark.

Mark: Thanks so much.

IPS: Good to hear your voice again Mark.

Frank: Good afternoon guys.

Lee: Yes, Hi Frank.

Frank: Lee, you're an inspiration to us all.

Lee: Oh. Thanks.

Frank: I just actually have one request: If you could just post a current newsletter to the Library or have it posted, so we just get an example of what you're saying to your clients. I'm just curious.

Lee: Okay. I can post one of them. If you probably wait about 30-days and let me post my new ones, I think that would be more revealing. Would that be okay?

Frank: Yes. Fine. That's perfectly okay.

Lee: Okay. I'll have that up probably within 30-days then Frank.

Frank: And Michael, thank you for going to a monthly publication of the newsletter. I was one of the guys that asked you do that. I appreciate you listening.

IPS: You bet. You bet. Hey, we listen to you.

Lee: That is a good thing, very good thing.

IPS: Alright. Everybody's happy about it. We're going to do a complete redesign of the NSACE site and a whole newsletter section. It's going to make it really easy for you guys to put up some great content. Alright. Lee. You know, as always, it's been a pleasure spending this time with you and I'm going to join with everybody else who's a Quantum Club™ member and say you're an inspiration to all of us, me included. And I'm honored that you're one of us and that I can count on you as a friend too, so thanks for sharing your time and your wisdom with us. We really appreciate it.

Lee: Well, thank you very much and thanks everybody for listening to me. I hope that you benefited as much as I enjoyed talking to you all.

IPS: You bet. Alright. Have a great day everybody! Love you all. Take care.

"Quantum Club has provided my agency with at least one new marketing program each year for the past three years. The result – I now spend four months each winter in Florida while the commission dollars pour in from those marketing programs. Cairnes-Tapley is on auto pilot. Thanks, Michael!"
~Peter Tapley, Jarrettsvile, MD

"I was shocked to discover how much time I wasted along with the un-harvested real agency dollars. You can teach an old dog new tricks. After 32 years in the insurance business I thought I had learned it all. NOT SO. Agency retention is up 1.5% overall. ROI from direct mail marketing has resulted in an average of 19 policies a month. Mountains of GREAT STUFF..."

Jamie Brown: Personal lines in Maryland

Jamie Brown, owns one of the most successful agencies in the history of State Farm and has been a Quantum Club™ member since 1993. He has been a Lifetime Member of State Farm's President's Club since 1996. He is a five-time State Farm Trophy winner and two-time winner of the Number One Auto Producer in the Country. Jamie has weaved Quantum Club principles and strategies throughout his entire agency making it one of the top 5 ranked auto and fire CheckPoint rankings as of May 2010. His bilingual staff cross-sells their clients and has wrote over 1,882 applications in the last 5 months and he has developed a Master Referral System that generates 20-30% of new production every month.

IPS: Good afternoon! I have on the line with me, Quantum Club member Jamie Brown who is an extremely successful State Farm agent in Maryland just outside the Washington DC area. Jamie has been with State Farm now for eighteen years, he was State Farm's number one auto producer in the country in 2005 and 2006, and he is a lifetime member of State Farm's President's Club, and he is a five time trophy winner. He certainly has enjoyed much success with State Farm and with the Quantum Club, and in life. I want to welcome Jamie on the call, how are you today Jamie?

Jamie Brown: Good, thanks you!

> "I've always been willing to learn, I've been a member of Quantum Club since 1993 and have put a lot of time or money in investing to make myself better, and learning from people like you...."

IPS: Before we get started, if you want to talk just a little bit about your agency, and then some of the things you feel make it successful. And then I've got some questions I want to ask you that I am sure our members are going to want to hear a lot about.

Jamie: Sure, I started back in February of 1992, I started it with one staff person and have grown it over the years and currently have sixteen staff members. We are now not only in the English market but also in the Hispanic market, eight of my staff are bi-lingual. Anything I market is primarily auto insurance, but then my staff does a very good job of pivoting to the other lines, the fire, life or health. So the big thing over the years is I've always been willing to learn, I've been a member of Quantum Club since 1993 and have put a lot of time or money in investing to make myself better, and learning from people like you, and just continuing to put money or reinvest money into the agency.

NICHE MARKETING

IPS: Excellent! We are going to talk more too, about the Hispanic market that you're servicing later in the call. I thought that it would be wise if we could maybe take a look right now at the success you're having with using cell service, or using cell phone numbers and texting to communicate with your clients. Now before we get into that I wanted to ask you a couple of questions. Do you use the text messaging for cold market, or cold calling or cold texting I guess you would call it?

Jamie: The only way we do it is if we buy an internet lead. What we have found is, the challenge from an internet lead is getting the person on the phone. So what we have found is that if you ask them a simple question: "John, is your Honda a 2 door or 4 door?" they start responding back and forth and you start building somewhat of a relationship and eventually they will talk to you. That has been the most success we've found working internet leads.

IPS: Okay, and is there a particular segment of the population that you find texting works better with?

Jamie: Well the studies have shown, you know obviously, if you are thirty years old or younger than thirty, the preferred method of communication now is texting. It's not phone calls, it's not e-mails, it is texting. They're definitely hot on that, but I have found, I'm 47 years old and I personally prefer to text rather than getting an e-mail, so it's starting to be more commonplace for all the generations.

IPS: Yes, I know if I want to communicate with my kids, the only way I'm going to get them is by texting it to them, I mean it just absolutely amazes me.

Jamie: Yes, I'll call their cell phone, they won't answer me, but if I send them a text they'll text me right back.

IPS: Yes, same thing and in funny language sometimes! You know, one of the things that I've actually recently discovered too, is that you can actually send a text to a land line.

Jamie: I did not realize that, that's pretty cool!

IPS: Yes it really is! We tested it yesterday and it works, it really does! What do you use the text messaging service for?

Jamie: We use a lot of it for primarily service on our current clients. We get what's called a beginning of day sheet and everything like that with late pays on it, and I have one lady that's kind of like called my bill collector and she'll just shoot an e-mail, or not only that but a text message also, "Please call me...(regarding whatever)" and so we use it for that, you know if we need little Johnny's driver's license number, we'll just shoot a text for that, we'll use it for confirming appointments, your imagination is the only limitation to how you can use it. What's really nice about the service is you can pre-schedule texts going out in the future so let's say I talked to you and I gave you an auto quote but I realized a ticket is going to fall off your record on November 15th, so I'm going to say John, I'm going to send you a text on November 16th, to call me because that's when I'm going to be able to give you the best rate. And I'll schedule it right now, it's going to go out on the 16th, and that's when you can call me.

IPS: That's excellent! I bet that really helps with your close ratio and new business?

Jamie: Yes, and then my staff, when they set up an appointment on Saturdays, before they leave the house they will go online and confirm the appointment texting with the client.

IPS: Excellent, because that's again, how the client prefers to communicate! When you get to be an old guy like me and you're going half blind, it gets to be tough to text, but I guess that's how everybody else does it.

Jamie: The name of the company is Message Media. You can create groups, you can download an excel spreadsheet with a list of phone numbers and names if you want, or you can enter them as individuals in alphabetical order. All I do is enter the cell number and the message. You are limited in characters so you can't make the message really long. Then I can schedule to send it not or at a later date. You can even track message delivery if I wanted.

IPS: So like zip drip, we can program these things to go out ahead of time...

Jamie: Exactly. It says: Your message will be sent to the following person, at this phone number; message sent. So it's just a confirmation real quick. Now the beauty of this is when I send that, and if I sent it, like for us, if I sent it from our State Farm computers it goes out, if the client replies back to it on my State Farm computer, then it comes in as an e-mail. It comes right back to the person who sent it.

IPS: And it's their phone number that's showing up in my email?

Jamie: Yes, exactly!

IPS: That's cool! And really your clients are thinking they are getting a personalized message from you.

Jamie: And you can even send these things out in groups; Happy Holidays, Happy Thanksgiving, you know just whatever; you're just thinking about them…

IPS: "John, please call regarding your auto insurance. Jamie." That's very cool, and I would imagine that people respond right back to these because that's how we handle texts.

Jamie: A lot of times we'll just text back and forth the messages if it's something simple, they won't even call you. So it is a very user friendly system that's allowing you to deliver an extra value to the customer. I don't think Geico and Progressive are going to be sitting there texting back and forth to the customer right now.

IPS: Last I knew, cave men weren't smart enough to use a cell phone so that probably sets you ahead of them! You know that's really one of the things that we as insurance agents need to do is deliver that extra value, and that's certainly one where you are doing that. Again, if somebody was interested in getting this service, could you give us the number and the person that they should ask for?

Jamie: Sure, the name of the company is Message Media the phone numbers is 866-751-8337, again 866-751-8337 and ask for Paul Diamond.

IPS: And should we mention your name or anything so they know who gets credit for the referrals?

Jamie: Paul Diamond, yes, if you mention my name I get a $20 referral fee so that's how that works. I paid $50 for the service, $50 a month and I have 18 staff using it.

IPS: And so do you pay $50 times 18 or do you pay $50 for just your agency?

Jamie: $50 just for my agency and every staff member has their own account.

IPS: Excellent…Jamie do you have templates?

Jamie: Yes, we save different templates, and different staff use different templates

IPS: And there are different messages, and then obviously you've got your bill collector and we know why you have her. Are there other specific uses that you use it for?

Jamie: We do, one of our staff, she sells a lot of life insurance so when we get the annual statement then she'll just send a text " I have great news for you, please call." And then she can go over their life statement with them.

IPS: That's great, and that's actually a tool that we could combine with using Quantum Quotes.

Jamie: I highly recommend using that service if you guys are not text messaging your clients.

IPS: I think we'll be signing up for it this afternoon! I see a tremendous potential for my entire operation, and I encourage the rest of the Quantum Club to do that. And remember when you call Paul Diamond at 866-751-8337, please mention Jamie's name and help our fellow Quantum Club member collect a whole stack of $20 bills!

Jamie: Thank you!

CROSS-SELLING

IPS: That brings me to the next thing I want to talk to you about. You have a reputation Jamie for having excellent cross sell strategies. I want you to tell us a little bit about how you are doing it, and why you are doing it.

Jamie: Well the number one reason is, I obviously want to maximize the amount of business I have per household. We know that out there every car has a home that is insured, and that every house is insured. So you know when we give somebody a quote for auto, we are assuming we are going to pick up their homeowner's insurance. The reason being is generally people are calling in is because of price, and the only way I can give them the best price is if I can give them the multiple line discount off of the house, and that's really a 17% discount. So we kind of have that discussion with the client and if you write the auto/home what you find out is that you really insulate your business. They are going to stay with you much longer than just a single line household like an auto or a home only. So my staff is trained to talk right away about the multi-line, and it's primarily we want the auto, and we want the house. If they don't own a house, then we'll do the auto and the renter's. And then the other piece, we run a lot of liability umbrella policies just because of the way our rating works with the multi line discount. So the insulation is huge plus this way we know our client is properly covered on our homeowner's piece there are a couple endorsements that we add; identity restoration, and sinkhole. We make it optional but we go over that. There house is their single largest investment, there are gaps in most homeowner's policies, we show them how we can cover the gap, and what it would cost them to cover.

> "So what I would encourage all the Quantum Club members to do is to take a drive around your local office area and just take a look. Who are the workers? Who are the landscapers? Who are the painters? Carpenters, who works at the convenience stores? And see if you have a market out there…The other thing, it's a very under-served market in a lot of areas. You could get into this market quickly and dominate it!"

IPS: So you take the focus away from price, even though that's why they had called.

Jamie: Exactly.

IPS: And I know a lot of the Quantum Club members who had been around this water cooler for awhile know about this study, maybe some of the newer members don't. State Farm had done a study a number of years ago that proved that more lines you have in a household, the longer the client will stay. Do you know some of the specifics of that?

Jamie: You know, the name of the company was Bane Company and they did the studies in the mid nineties or right around 1995. The main message was simply, the more lines of business you have with a client, the longer they are going to stay with you. Auto and Home, then if you add the Life policy it went up tremendously.

IPS: Exactly, and as you had pointed out to me when we had spoke the other day, you are keeping the other agents out of your households.

Jamie: Correct, if I have your house insured, and another agent has your auto, you are generally calling that other agent all the time regarding your auto; change of vehicle, bought a new car or whatever. You are going to have more discussions there and sooner or later someone is going to get smart at that agency and say "John, we don't have your house, how about if I give you a quote on the house?" So your discussions with the other agent, it almost promotes defection from your agency.

BILINGUAL

IPS: When we talked, you had mentioned that half of your staff is bilingual; English and Spanish. I know you've been focusing on the Hispanic market for the last five years. Can you tell us a little bit about what you're seeing trend wise as far as growth in the Hispanic marketplace, and what you're doing to take advantage of that?

Jamie: Yes, the growth in my area, it happened overnight, it was huge. And I think in a lot of different cities in the country it's also happening. What happens is that you don't recognize it until it's almost too late. The way I recognized it was, if I went to a convenience store, or a McDonald's or a fast food store...back in 2002,03,04, primarily most of those workers were African American. When I went in 2005, I noticed within like a twelve month period of time, it shifted from African American to Hispanic, so a lot of the blue collar force in my area is Hispanic now. And what happens is, Hispanic families generally will move into one area because family is big for them, and they like to have a lot of their children go to the same schools; and so they'll come in and dominate an area pretty quickly. And a lot of times before you recognize it, they have been there for years. . Back in July I hired three bilingual staff at one time, I interviewed one lady, and I said you start in two weeks provided you can send me enough people where I can hire two other people. So she sent me a bunch of her friends, so I hired three at one time because if one was away on a vacation or out to lunch I didn't want to have to speak Spanish; I don't speak a lick of Spanish. So, I hired three at one time, and now I'm up to eight.

IPS: Senor that makes a lot of sense!

> "They are going to stay with you much longer than just a single line household like an auto or a home only."

Jamie: That's the same thing here, if I am interviewing somebody and I have candidate A and candidate B and they are exactly the same with the exception of one speaks just English, and one speaks English and Spanish, well that extra skill set, the one that speaks Spanish, they're going to get the nod for the job. It gives me more flexibility.

IPS: How big is, as far as using Spanish in your marketing, do you use it any differently in marketing than when you market to the English marketplace?

Jamie: On my direct mail, no because I have pieces through State Farm that are bilingual pieces; English on one side, and Spanish on the other. But what's really big in the Hispanic market, bigger than most, are the referrals. So I did a focus group study back in 2005 with a television company because I was thinking about doing TV advertising, and you know we had a room full of about forty Hispanics and we sat and asked questions. I asked them "How far would you drive to purchase insurance form somebody?" And the distance was almost an hour; it was longer than that if they trusted you spoke their language. That gets me a pretty good radius. So you know if you insure them, and you do a good job and they like you, then they are going to send their brother, their mother, their sister, their cousin, their uncle.

IPS: I have witnessed the exact same thing. Instead of actually making the referral, they will actually bring them to the office.

Jamie: Yes, they walk them in, it is amazing!

LOST SOULS

IPS: It is an incredible thing, it really says a lot about your agency. Now the other source of business that you've had some experience with is internet leads. Can you tell us a little bit about your take on internet leads because it's , I think a little different than what most agents do and I think I agree with you 100%.

Jamie: Yes, what I do is back in 2008, I strictly did internet leads and what I did is stopped my direct mail; and that was kind of a strategic error. What I've found is, the internet business has gotten really sleazy, in other words all these internet companies, if they don't sell the lead, they'll turn around and sell the lead to another company that's in the same business. So if you are buying leads from several different companies you can actually be buying the same lead three, four, five different times. And the lead isn't as, sometimes as fresh as you think it is. It's not like the person was just on the computer, you know they've resold it to another internet lead company so it may be an hour old, you have no idea. What we have found is, especially auto insurance. Most agents, or agencies or companies are buying all the auto leads so they would sell up to seven or eight times. So all of a sudden you are in a battle with five other carriers or companies calling this client, and after they get one, two or three phone calls they are done with it! They are confused, tired of talking to people, got what they want, or just not interested!

IPS: Because the consumer has no idea they are going to be hearing from several different people.

Jamie: Exactly, so we have paid on the average $10-$12 a lead and it was a huge battle, so I was like "Why don't we work these things as if they were old?" We work them 60-90 days old so once it's 60 days old, if we call the client and we can get into a conversation with them, they'll talk to us now simply because no one else is talking to them. And so I am out of that rat race of competing with all those other calls.

IPS: So in those first few days while the lead is fresh it's almost like the consumer has been in a rat race with all of these people calling them on the phone and they've gotten over being mad about it by the time you get around to calling them.

Jamie: Yes, 60-90 days later now they've got time to sit down and talk about it. And you know some will listen to you, some won't, but it's a much better process than calling them right away. Now the other thing I do is, because the auto lead is always the hot lead and other people are always competing against all the other agencies that way; I stopped buying those, and I started buying renters and homeowners leads. We would pivot from the renters and home leads to an auto.

IPS: And that really works with your overall strategy of getting the entire account, and you're talking to them about something that everybody else wants to talk about.

Jamie: Exactly, now there's an internet lead company that I just got an email from earlier this week that sells what they call 'aged leads', and they are advertising it for a buck a piece, which is a lot better than what I was paying. And that company name is Link First Solutions, I haven't talked to them yet, but I am reading the email. That phone number is 888-480-7556, and they are advertising aged auto, home and life leads at a greatly reduced price and they are saying it's a buck a piece. And again, the phone number is 888-480-7556.

IPS: That's a bargain! And do you know with these aged leads if they are X dated by any chance?

Jamie: I have no idea, like I said I haven't talked to them.

DIRECT MAIL

IPS: I have a suspicion their phones are probably going to be busy this afternoon thank you for that lead! And you had mentioned that you took a break in your direct mail campaign, and I believe you've been using direct mail since almost day one back in 1993. Can you tell us a little bit about what you are doing in direct mail?

Jamie: Yes, basically I've tested all kinds of direct mail over eighteen years, the only thing that seems to make my phone ring is a marketing piece regarding auto insurance. specifically the price. Now what I'm sending right now is everything through State farm because it's co-op'd so heavily. What I do is, I'm buying about 64,000 names over the year, and the primary zip codes that I market to are within ten miles of my office. And I mail them where State Farm has a program going on in my office where I am hitting them up eight times over the next 12 months.

IPS: So they hear from you about every six and a half weeks or so? So your name is always fresh in their minds, they know who they are hearing from. Unlike a lot of us who are independent agents, we can use a lot of far out marketing pieces that we want to use. So do you have to use State Farm compliant pieces?

Jamie: Yes, everything I use I just order it through corporate and they just send it out.

IPS: Okay so you do nothing other than write a check or debit it right out of your commission statement?

Jamie: Correct, I go on and order the leads and they take it right out of my check.

> "If the insurance company sees that you're doing high impact marketing and you write a lot of good quality business they're going to be more than happy to talk to you about co-op dollars."

IPS: Now, you're using the co-op, and that's money that so many agents leave laying on the table. You're using co-op dollars to do this? Are you doing anything to get yourself enhanced co-op contracts or offers from State Farm?

Jamie: Well each zone and State Farm is kind of different, so I get the same deal any other agent gets. I know in the independent world, you have different companies that want a different volume of business, so I believe you can almost talk to your relationship person with that carrier and somewhat negotiate with those possible co-op dollars.

IPS: Yes you certainly can and that was the point I wanted to drive home. I realize you are the person we are interviewing today, but what you do you do with State Farm. Most of our members are independent agents and you can negotiate with a lot of these IA carriers and get yourself additional co-op ad money.

Jamie: That's free dollars, you should take every one, I mean.

IPS: Absolutely! Especially, when we're in a marketplace where everybody is looking for more business. If the insurance company sees that you're doing high impact marketing and you write a lot of good quality business they're going to be more than happy to talk to you about co-op dollars. Well Jamie, we have come pretty close to the end of my list, and before we open it up for Q& A is there anything else you'd like to add?

Jamie: Nothing, I think that we pretty much covered everything.

IPS: Okay, well if you think of anything you can always text.

Rusty: Hey Jamie, how you all doing?

Jamie: Good, how are you?

Rusty: I am doing great, this is all very cool stuff. I am curious about the direct mail, sending eight pieces out in twelve months. I notice in my mailbox at home, I am getting a State Farm agents campaign, it appears to be the same type of stuff. What kind of response rate have you gotten on that? What kind of results have you seen?

Jamie: Every zone is different on what they are sending out and how it's going, so to tell you exactly what response rate you are getting based on that one I honestly have no idea. You know I can tell you this, any great direct mail campaign 1% is like ideal. You know I can tell you it's less than 1%. I think part of the magic is hey if you're hitting them up every 6 ½ weeks, hopefully you're going to hit them sometime during that year when they have their insurance bill still in their hand or their current company just kind of pissed them off so the constant philosophy is just being in front of them. And State Farm is big about branding so it's also the branding message that they are sending out.

Rusty: Got it, okay.

IPS: While Rusty is still on the line, Rusty and his partner Jimmy are one of our Agency Mastery Program (AMP) clients this year which is another service provided by Insurance Profit Systems. One of the things that Rusty has done very successfully is , one of the many things they've done very successfully is working internet leads. A lot of people buy the things and they don't work them. And I suspect Rusty wrote Link First Solution's name down and I think Jimmy is probably on the other line talking to them right now ,so much success with that one! I am sure you'll chase those down quickly! All right, Good, nice to talk to you Rusty!

Rusty: Thanks Guys!

> "You're going to make some money. You're going to enjoy some business and you will have some time with your family. That's the main thing."
> ~Stan Eden, Ft. Smith, AR

> "Best information I have ever received. This will dramatically change the way our agency operates."
> -Darren Vermost, Clearwater, FL

> "This absolutely fantastic! It is so chock-full of value that you can't put a price on it! These phenomenally successful agents have peeled back the curtains on what they have done to reach this pinnacle state in the industry. They reveal step-by-step their best kept secrets, and share with the world instead of just keeping them to themselves. Anyone who reads this will discover exactly what it takes to explode their practice and the fastest way possible."
> ~Brian Anastasio, State Farm Insurance, Albuquerque, NM

"I was shocked to discover how much time I wasted along with the un-harvested real agency dollars. You can teach an old dog new tricks. After 32 years in the insurance business I thought I had learned it all. NOT SO. Agency retention is up 1.5% overall. ROI from direct mail marketing has resulted in an average of 19 policies a month. Mountains of GREAT STUFF…"
~Bill Holland, Savannah, GA

"Quantum Club is an essential tool in my agency. Quantum Club has so much to choose from – something for everyone. If you're not a Quantum Clubber you are handicapping yourself for life. Quantum Club has changed my agency, my life and my lifestyle – thanks a million!"
~Mark Helfrich, Middleton, WI

"Quantum Club has changed my business completely. I can see the growth every month in my commission checks and the quality of clients I am getting. This is without a doubt the best thing I have ever done in business."
~John Obrey, Derry, NE

"In my four years as a Quantum Club member my agency revenue is up 191%! Quantum Club is the greatest professional organization I have ever been associated with. Put me down as a lifetime member!!"
~J.D. Dickinson, Post Falls, ID

"Took eight weeks of vacation this past year (usually took a week before). Income has increased over 30% in the past 3 years. My client numbers have not increased much but the number of policies in each account has dramatically increased. This past year was my best in 42 years by a wide margin."
~ Lew Doubleday, Ankeny, IA

"I <u>originally joined because I thought I would join for a few months, get all the free stuff, then quit.</u> A light came on. After receiving the materials I realized with Quantum Club I would get coaching on how to build my agency so in 5 years be able to sell it (if I choose) and get the most out of it, or build it to where I could take vacation and it would grow. I don't have to run 100 miles an hour for the rest of my life!"
~David Bybee, Anderson, IN

"Since joining IPS, I'm down to a 40-hour work week and have gained a lot of control over my life. I still have farther to go – but now I have direction and a plan to get there."
~Karen Delewski, Wyomissing, PA

"Thank you for giving me the big picture on how to look at this business."
~Jerry Molfetas, St. Petersburg, FL

"After joining the Quantum Club just before Boot Camp 2002 I came to Boot Camp and left with a 3 year goal – "Get my wife to quit work and be home with my boys." Thanks to you this 3 year goal was made in 1 year!"
~Russ Castle, Redwood City, CA

"WOW!! Jammed pack with everything you need to get your marketing up and running to make money fast. I learned more in one day about marketing insurance than I have in the 20 years I have been in this business learning concepts from the so-called insurance professionals. Thanks Michael."
~Dennis Pfauth, Longmont, CO

"We are fortunate to advise still in swamped status because of high impact. Net profit last month up at least 251% over same month prior year. My biggest problem is what do I do with the money so Sam doesn't get it. Time is still a large challenge but nothing in comparison to what it was one year ago and was for more than 12 years when I did nothing but waste time. I feel more organized and in control than ever…The numbers are in and they don't lie –

- Record number of new apps in July: 71
- Personal Lines new volume: $52,977
- Commercial Lines new volume: $68,272

We are focused because we have a source that helps us keep our priorities straight, writing profitable new business, weeding out the unprofitable and having fun."
~Mike Stromsoe, Temecula, CA

"I have one year under my belt with Quantum Club. By making a few changes, **my agency's net income is up 43%.** I can't wait for the next 12 months."
~Steve Barrick, Hanover, PA

> "You're going to make some money. You're going to enjoy some business and you will have some time with your family. That's the main thing."
> ~Stan Eden, Ft. Smith, AR

> "Stress, worries, long hours of work – GONE. <u>More control, more time off, more money. Only possible through IPS</u> – Quantum Club. I cannot believe that an agent can survive without your knowledge and seminars. The future of a successful agency is only available through your research and knowledge."
> ~Mark Davidson, Lincoln, NE

> "I only wish that I had done this years ago. My mindset about this industry has been totally changed. Thank you Michael Jans."
> ~Art Rhodes, LaGrande, OR

> "Invaluable information, techniques and media to take your business to the next level. Taught by people who are actually involved in the industry and who are achieving astounding things with the tools that Michael Jans has developed."
> ~Jim Bruton, Ukiah, CA

> "Michael, You're a great guy, and I appreciate all I have learned through your many avenues you make available to us. That being said, if you dropped dead tomorrow I'd still be in the "Q" Club. The invaluable insight and phenomenal marketing brain power in this group makes it the "deal of the century" by itself. Thank You!"
> ~Terry Ward, Shelby, NC

FILE ORGANIZATION + FILING
PLANTS, COFFEE, DUST
SHREDDING
OFFICE MGT
SUPPLIES & CLOSET ORGANIZING
COMPANY MATERIALS
TELEPHONE ASSISTANCE
LUNCH RUN
P.O. — MAIL OPENING

BOOKKEEPING
   PAYABLES
   OFFICE EXPENSES

MARKETING
   COORDINATE WITH KIM
   DEVELOP MATERIALS

TRACKING
   NEW, LOST
   REFERRALS
   NICHES
   NETWORKING